The Crofters (Scotland)

ISBN 0 41401087 6

A catalogue record for this
book is available from the
British Library

The Crofters (Scotland) Act 1993

Derek Flyn and Keith H. R. Graham

W.GREEN/Sweet & Maxwell

EDINBURGH

1994

CONTENTS

Page

CROFTERS (SCOTLAND) ACT 1993*

(1993 c. 44)

[A Table showing the derivation of the provisions of this consolidation Act will be found at the end of the Act. The Table has no official status.]

ARRANGEMENT OF SECTIONS

---

* Annotations by Derek Flyn, LL.B., Solicitor in Private Practice, and Keith H. R. Graham, LL.B., W.S., Principal Clerk of the Scottish Land Court.

An Act to consolidate certain enactments relating to crofting, with amendments to give effect to recommendations of the Scottish Law Commission.

[5th November 1993]

PARLIAMENTARY DEBATES
Hansard, H.L. Vol. 546, col. 1221.

The Joint Committee on Consolidation Bills on June 16, 1993 considered the Crofters (Scotland) Bill along with the Report of the Scottish Law Commission on the Bill (Cm. 2187). Apart from not approving one recommendation on the grounds that the matter was currently before the Land Court and disagreeing with an amendment to improve the form of the Bill, the Committee were satisfied that the Law Commission's recommendations were necessary for providing a satisfactory consolidation of the law.

INTRODUCTION AND GENERAL NOTE

This long-awaited consolidation of the Crofting Acts extends to Scotland only and deals with certain holdings of land in the "crofting counties", *i.e.* the former counties of Argyll, Caithness, Inverness, Orkney, Ross & Cromarty, Sutherland and Zetland.

The history of crofting tenure (which applies only to the Highlands and Islands of Scotland) is long and complicated and has received much attention in recent years. Its introduction was the product of various factors. The public sympathy aroused during the investigations of the Napier Commission in 1883 and the subsequent widespread debate, coupled with the extension of the parliamentary franchise in 1885, resulted in the introduction of a statutory code by means of the Crofters Holdings (Scotland) Act 1886 which established the first Crofters Commission.

This unique form of land tenure remains founded on the same three principles as it did when it was introduced in 1886: (a) security of tenure subject to compliance with standard conditions of tenancy; (b) the right to a fair rent for the duration of the tenancy; and (c) compensation for any permanent improvements provided by the tenant or his predecessors in the tenancy and left by him at the termination of the tenancy.

The effect of the statutory protection was to render written leases with crofting tenants unnecessary and they remain unusual. Although the remedy was designed to protect certain occupiers of lands, it has now developed into a peculiarly complex system of statutory rules which controls the use of certain lands and allows those involved easy access to a specialised tribunal, the Scottish Land Court.

The original Crofters Commission was appointed to administer the Crofters Holdings (Scotland) Act 1886. The first few years were mainly spent fixing fair rents (which are still subject to possible revision every seven years) and dealing with any arrears of rent which the Commission were empowered to reduce or cancel. Gradually the Commission developed into a quasi-judicial body dealing with many issues, such as boundary disputes and other questions affecting crofting rights. When the first Commission was dissolved in 1912, much case law had been recorded in its 25 annual reports along with a wealth of information about the holdings themselves. This information can still be resorted to in the case of a dispute.

With the introduction of the Small Landholders (Scotland) Act 1911, the first Crofters Commission was superseded by the Scottish Land Court and the rights given to crofters in 1886 were extended to cover small agricultural tenants throughout Scotland. Two classes of such tenants were recognised: landholders and statutory small tenants. In 1955 the first Crofters (Scotland) Act, while leaving untouched the two categories of landholder and statutory small tenant in the non-crofting counties, re-established the category of crofter in the seven crofting counties; a second Crofters Commission was established which continues to exist, its function being broadly administrative as against the Scottish Land Court's continuing judicial function.

In addition, the crofter's limited right to control the future of his tenancy by assignation or testate succession combined with rights introduced in 1976 to acquire an owner's title or to share in the value of any land taken from him for development has expanded the crofter's interest in his subjects into a form of property. Likewise, the close scrutiny of government agencies including the dedicated Crofters Commission and the expert Land Court gives the subjects themselves a singular protection.

The complexity of the law applicable to crofting subjects has long been open to criticism. The law itself and its administration may have hindered crofters in the past from realising the potential of their crofts and prevented them from benefitting from opportunities for development such as afforestation and fish-farming. However, recent changes such as the right to buy and crofter forestry suggest that crofters' rights in their lands are unlikely to diminish.

The question whether a holding constitutes a croft (or indeed whether any land is subject to crofting controls) can be a difficult matter. This can be determined by the Land Court which has jurisdiction in such matters (s.53).

The fact that a holding has been registered as a croft in the Register of Crofts is purely administrative and does not prove the holding is a croft (*Elder* v. *Manson* 1964 S.L.T. (Land Ct.) 15.

In his article "When is a croft not a croft" (1991) JLSS 115, Sir Crispin Agnew of Lochnaw, Bt., Advocate, illustrates how the status of a holding may be examined to discover if it is a croft and what sources of evidence may be available.

ABBREVIATIONS

　The 1955 Act: The Crofters (Scotland) Act 1955.
　The 1961 Act: The Crofters (Scotland) Act 1961.
　The 1976 Act: The Crofting Reform (Scotland) Act 1976.
　The 1991 Act: The Crofter Forestry (Scotland) Act 1991.

DEFINITIONS

　These words are used throughout this Act.
　"cottar": s.12(5).
　"croft": s.3(1).
　"crofter": s.3(3).
　"crofting counties": s.61(1).
　"croft land": s.12(3).
　"landlord": s.61(1).
　"Martinmas": s.61(1).
　"permanent improvement": s.30(7) and Sched. 2.
　"the Register of Crofts": s.41.
　"Whitsunday": s.61(1).

The Crofters Commission

Constitution and general functions of Crofters Commission

　1.—(1) The Crofters Commission ("the Commission") established by section 1 of the 1955 Act shall continue in being.

　(2) The Commission shall have the functions of reorganising, developing and regulating crofting in the crofting counties of Scotland, of promoting the interests of crofters there and of keeping under review matters relating to crofting, and such other functions as are conferred on them by or under this Act.

　(3) The Commission shall carry out their functions in accordance with such directions of a general character as may be given by the Secretary of State and in carrying out their functions shall have regard to local circumstances and conditions.

　(4) The Commission shall consist of not more than 9 members appointed by the Secretary of State, and of the members one shall be appointed by the Secretary of State to be chairman of the Commission.

　(5) The Commission shall include members with knowledge of crofting conditions and at least one member who can speak the Gaelic language.

　(6) The provisions contained in Schedule 1 to this Act shall have effect in relation to the Commission.

DEFINITIONS

　"crofter": s.3(3).
　"crofting counties": s.61(1).

GENERAL NOTE

　The present Crofters Commission is the second body of that name (see the Introduction and General Note); it has its offices at 4/6 Castle Wynd, Inverness.

Particular powers and duties of the Commission

　2.—(1) In the exercise of their general functions of reorganising, developing and regulating crofting, it shall be the duty of the Commission—

　　(a)　to keep under general review all matters relating to crofts and crofting conditions, including, without prejudice to the foregoing generality, land settlement, the improvement of land and livestock, the planting of trees, the supply of agricultural equipment and requisites, the marketing of agricultural produce, experimental work on crofting methods, the provision of demonstration crofts, the needs of the crofting communities for public services of all kinds, the provision of social amenities and the need for industries to provide supplementary occupations for crofters or work for their families; and to make such recommendations as they may think fit on any of the matters aforesaid;

(b) to collaborate so far as their powers and duties permit with any body or person in the carrying out of any measures for the economic development and social improvement of the crofting counties;

(c) to advise the Secretary of State on any matter relating to crofts and crofting conditions which he may refer to them, or on which they may think fit to submit advice to him;

(d) to exercise the powers conferred on them by this Act in such manner as may seem to them in each case desirable.

(2) For the purpose of assisting them in the local execution of their functions under this Act, the Commission shall have power to appoint a panel of suitable persons resident in the crofting counties to act as assessors, when required by the Commission so to act, and may make to such assessors in respect of any loss of earnings they would otherwise have made or any additional expenses (including travelling and subsistence expenses) to which they would not otherwise have been subject, being loss or expenses necessarily suffered or incurred by them for the purpose of enabling them to perform duties as such assessors, such payments as the Secretary of State may, with the approval of the Treasury, determine.

(3) The Commission shall send to the principal clerk of the Land Court to be recorded in the Crofters Holdings Book every order, determination, consent, authorisation or other proceeding of theirs which they may think proper to be recorded therein.

(4) The Commission shall make an annual report to the Secretary of State on the exercise and performance by them of their functions under this Act and the Secretary of State shall lay a copy of the report before each House of Parliament, together with such comments as he may think fit to make.

GENERAL NOTE

Under its own rules of procedure, the Crofters Commission's business is to be carried out in a simple and orderly manner and as free from formality as is consistent with efficient administration.

The Commission may refer to the Land Court questions of fact or law arising under the Act in any application or other proceeding before the Commission (s.53(1)). It must send information to the Land Court for recording (subs. (3)) and is to receive intimation of the Land Court's determination of any question coming before it under the Act (s.53(2)).

An annual report is issued by the Commission after each calendar year.

Meaning of croft and crofter

Meaning of croft and crofter

3.—(1) Subject to subsection (2) below, in this Act "croft" means—

(a) as from 1st October 1955, every holding (whether occupied by a landholder or not) situated in the crofting counties to which any of the provisions of the Small Landholders (Scotland) Acts 1886 to 1931 relating to landholders applied;

(b) as from 1st October 1955, every holding situated as aforesaid to which section 32 of the Small Landholders (Scotland) Act 1911 applied (statutory small tenants);

(c) as from the date of registration, every holding situated as aforesaid which was constituted a croft by the registration of the tenant thereof as a crofter in the Crofters Holdings Book under section 4 of the 1955 Act;

   (d) as from the date of the direction, every holding situated as aforesaid which was constituted a croft by a direction of the Secretary of State under section 2(1) of the 1961 Act;

   (e) as from the date of entry, every holding entered in the register of crofts by the Commission in accordance with their decision under section 15(4) of the 1955 Act where—

      (i) the decision was notified to the landlord and the tenant of the holding; and

      (ii) neither the landlord nor the tenant successfully challenged the decision on an application for a declarator as to the status of the tenant made to the Land Court within 2 months of the giving of such notification.

(2) Subsection (1) above is without prejudice to the effect of—

   (a) section 24(1) of this Act and the corresponding provision of the 1955 Act which is repealed by this Act (that is to say section 12(4));

   (b) a direction under section 24(2) or (3) of this Act and the corresponding provisions of the 1955 Act which are repealed by this Act (that is to say section 16(7) or (9)).

(3) In this Act "crofter" means the tenant of a croft.

(4) For the purposes of this Act—

   (a) any right in pasture or grazing land held or to be held by the tenant of a croft, whether alone or in common with others, and

   (b) any land comprising any part of a common grazing which has been apportioned for the exclusive use of a crofter under section 52(4) of this Act, and,

   (c) any land held runrig which has been apportioned under section 52(8) of this Act,

shall be deemed to form part of the croft.

(5) For the purposes of this Act, where—

   (a) a crofter has acquired his entire croft other than any such right or land as is referred to in subsection (4) above; or

   (b) any person, not being a crofter, has obtained an apportionment of any land under section 52 of this Act,

then the person referred to in paragraph (a) or (b) above shall be deemed to hold the right or land referred to therein in tenancy until held otherwise and that right or land shall be deemed to be a croft.

GENERAL NOTE

   When the 1886 Act created crofting tenure, the method used was to standardise the occupier's rights so that any occupier of land who qualified as a "crofter" was given protection. The 1886 Act defined the crofter's holding as any piece of land consisting of arable or pasture land held by the crofter alone or in common. It included the site of his dwelling-house. Subsequently it was the land itself which was given statutory protection. As there was nothing in the 1886 Act to prevent a crofter's holding from falling out of the Act if it became vacant, the history of the holding and its tenants may be important.

   The 1886 Act thus gave the word "crofter" a special meaning but this was lost to the Statute Book on the introduction of the Small Landholders (Scotland) Act 1911, which applied a crofting-type tenure to small-holdings throughout Scotland. Indeed the 1911 Act was directed to be read and construed with the "Crofters Acts" defined as meaning the Acts of 1886, 1887, 1891 and 1908. These four Acts and the 1911 Act were cited together as the "Small Landholders (Scotland) Acts, 1886 to 1911". New terms "landholder" and "statutory small tenant" were introduced to describe the protected tenant, then to be found throughout Scotland.

   The Crofters (Scotland) Act 1955 re-introduced the term "crofter" to the crofting counties and the protected holding was designated a "croft". Care should be taken to ensure that the subjects described and the occupiers thereof are indeed within the statutory definitions. The words are frequently used elsewhere (the Court of Session in *Fearnan Partnership* v. *Grindlay* ([2nd Div.] 1990 S.L.T. 704), discuss without comment "crofters" and "crofts" in an area outside the crofting counties).

Enlargement of crofts

Enlargement where owner and crofter are in agreement

4.—(1) Where the owner of any land which is not itself a croft and which does not form part of a croft agrees to grant a tenancy of such land to any crofter, then—

(a) except in such a case as is mentioned in paragraph (b) below, if the owner of the said land and the crofter agree that such land will form part of any croft of which the crofter is tenant, the land shall, as from the date of entry under the said tenancy, form part of such croft and this Act shall apply accordingly to the croft as so enlarged,

(b) in a case where the area of the croft (exclusive of any common pasture or grazing land held therewith) together with the area of the land exceeds 30 hectares and the rent of the croft together with the rent under the said tenancy exceeds £100, the Commission may, on an application being made to them jointly by the owner of the land and the crofter, direct that the land shall form part of the croft and, if they make such direction, then as from the date of the direction or the date of entry under the said tenancy, whichever is the later, the land shall form part of the croft, and this Act so far as relating to crofting shall apply accordingly to the croft as so enlarged.

(2) The Commission shall make a direction under subsection (1)(b) above only if they are satisfied that such a direction—

(a) would be of benefit to the croft; and

(b) would not result in the croft as enlarged by the land referred to in that subsection being substantially larger than 30 hectares or capable of being let as a croft at an annual rent substantially in excess of £100.

(3) Where any such land as is mentioned in section 38(3)(a) of this Act is included in a reorganisation scheme made under that section and confirmed by the Secretary of State, then as from the date on which the scheme is put into effect this Act shall apply to such land.

(4) The owner of any land which becomes part of a croft by virtue of subsection (1)(a) above shall give notice to the Commission of the enlargement of such croft.

GENERAL NOTE

This section provides for enlarging existing crofts and common grazings by agreement between the landowner and the crofter(s). Older enactments are still available, which permit the enlargement of a croft by direction of the Secretary of State on the application of the tenant, although the process is obsolescent. A reorganisation scheme may permit the Commission to direct land to be used for enlargement (see subs. (3)).

The conditions of tenure

The statutory conditions

5.—(1) Every tenancy of a croft shall be subject to the conditions set out in Schedule 2 to this Act (in this Act referred to as "the statutory conditions").

(2) A crofter shall not be subject to be removed from the croft of which he is tenant except—

(a) where one year's rent of the croft is unpaid;

(b) in consequence of the breach of one or more of the statutory conditions, other than the condition as to payment of rent; or

(c) in pursuance of any enactment, including any enactment contained in this Act.

(3) Any contract or agreement made by a crofter by virtue of which he is deprived of any right conferred on him by any provision of this Act (other than sections 12 to 19, 21 and 37) shall to that extent be void unless the contract or agreement is approved by the Land Court.

GENERAL NOTE
For the first time the statutory conditions of tenure are stated in a positive manner. The crofter's tenure of his croft has long been described as that of a tenant from year to year and his conditions of tenancy have been laid down in a series of Acts commencing with the Crofters Holdings (Scotland) Act 1886; the most recent is the Crofter Forestry (Scotland) Act 1991. Despite this description, a crofter's right to his tenancy should now be considered as a form of quasi-ownership.

A crofter may be removed by the Land Court on application by the landlord where one year's rent is unpaid or for the breach of one or more of the statutory conditions of tenure (see s.26(1)). These statutory conditions are now set out in Sched. 2. However, where a breach of the statutory conditions is capable of being remedied, the Land Court will allow the defaulting tenant an opportunity of remedying the breach (see, *e.g. Corbett* v. *MacLeod* 1990 S.L.C.R. 25).

The effect of the Land Court's approval in terms of subs. (3) has been considered in *Stornoway Trust* v. *Mackay* 1989 S.L.T. (Land Ct.) 36. (See also *Hamilton* v. *Noble* 1989 S.L.C.R. 51). Such approval should be sought on an application form (general) available from the Scottish Land Court, 1 Grosvenor Crescent, Edinburgh.

Rent

6.—(1) The rent payable by a crofter as one of the statutory conditions shall be the yearly rent, including money and any prestations other than money, payable for the year current at the commencement of this Act or, in the case of a croft let after the commencement of this Act, fixed at the date of the letting, unless and until that rent is altered in accordance with the provisions of this Act.

(2) The rent may be altered by agreement in writing between the landlord and the crofter to such amount and for such period as may be so agreed; and thereupon the rent so agreed shall be the rent payable by the crofter so long as the agreement subsists and thereafter so long as—

(a) no new agreement between the landlord and the crofter shall have been made; or

(b) no different rent shall have been fixed by the Land Court under this Act.

(3) The Land Court may, on the application of the crofter or the landlord, determine what is a fair rent to be paid by the crofter to the landlord for the croft, and may pronounce an order accordingly; and the rent so fixed by the Land Court shall be the rent payable by the crofter as from the first term of Whitsunday or Martinmas next succeeding the decision of the Land Court:
Provided that—

(a) where the rent payable for the croft has been fixed by the Land Court it shall not be altered, except by mutual agreement between the crofter and the landlord, for a period of 7 years from the term at which it first became payable; and

(b) where a croft is let after the commencement of this Act, the rent shall not be altered by the Land Court for a period of 7 years from the term at which it first became payable or for such longer period as may have been agreed upon between the crofter and the landlord.

(4) Before determining what is a fair rent for a croft, the Land Court shall hear the parties and shall take into consideration all the circumstances of the case, of the croft and of the district, and in particular shall take into consideration any permanent or unexhausted improvements on the croft and suitable thereto which have been executed or paid for by the crofter or his predecessors in the tenancy.

GENERAL NOTE
The forms to be used when applying to have fair rents determined under subs. (3) are available from the Scottish Land Court, 1 Grosvenor Crescent, Edinburgh.

For the principles of fair renting it is necessary to examine observations made by the Land

Court in a lengthy series of cases, including *MacAlpin* v. *Duke of Hamilton's Trustees* (1914) 2 S.L.C.R. 74 at 82 and *Secretary of State for Scotland* v. *Ramage* (1952) 40 S.L.C.R. 29.

Renunciation of tenancy

7.—(1) A crofter shall be entitled, on one year's notice in writing to the landlord, to renounce his tenancy as at any term of Whitsunday or Martinmas.

(2) If a crofter renounces his tenancy the landlord shall be entitled to set off all rent due or to become due against any sum found to be due by the landlord to the crofter or to the Secretary of State by way of compensation for permanent improvements made on the croft.

DEFINITIONS
"compensation for permanent improvements": s.30.

Assignation of croft

8.—(1) A crofter shall not assign his croft—
(a) to a member of his family unless he obtains the consent in writing of his landlord or, failing such consent, the consent in writing of the Commission on an application made to them;
(b) to a person other than a member of his family unless he obtains the consent in writing of the Commission on an application made to them.

(2) A landlord who has given his consent in pursuance of subsection (1)(a) above shall notify the Commission of the assignation and the name of the assignee.

(3) The Commission shall give notice to the landlord of any application made to them for their consent to the assignation of the tenancy of a croft and before deciding whether to give or to withhold their consent shall afford to the crofter and to the landlord an opportunity of making representations to them.

(4) In considering any application made as aforesaid the Commission shall take into account the family and other circumstances of the crofter and of the proposed assignee of the croft and the general interests of the township in which the croft is situated.

(5) Where a crofter assigns his croft otherwise than with the consent in writing of the Commission in a case where he is required to obtain such consent in pursuance of subsection (1) above, such assignation and any deed purporting so to assign the tenancy shall be null and void and the Commission may declare the croft to be vacant.

(6) An assignation to which the Commission have given their consent under this section shall take effect at the term of Whitsunday or Martinmas first occurring not less than two months after the date on which such consent was intimated to the crofter, unless before the said term of Whitsunday or Martinmas, as the case may be, the crofter or his executor or legatee and the assignee jointly give to the Commission notice in writing that they do not intend to proceed with the assignation.

(7) Any reference in this section to a croft shall include a reference to a part of a croft, being a part consisting of any right in pasture or grazing land deemed by virtue of section 3(4) of this Act to form part of a croft.

DEFINITIONS
"Martinmas": s.61(1).
"member of the crofter's family": s.61(2).
"Whitsunday": s.61(1).

GENERAL NOTE
An application by a crofter to "assign his croft" implies a transfer by him of his whole interest in the tenancy. The permanent improvements provided by the crofter and his predecessors in the tenancy will transfer with the right to the tenancy. The assignee may therefore be acquiring a

considerable asset, including the croft house. It will then be open to him to exercise rights to acquire an owner's title (see s.12).

Consent of the Commission is only required: (i) where the crofter wishes to assign to a member of his family and the landlord fails to give his written consent or (ii) in the event of the crofter wishing to assign to a person outside his family.

The forms to be used when applying for consent to assign the tenancy of a croft are available from the Crofters Commission, 4/6 Castle Wynd, Inverness.

Sub-division of croft

9. A crofter shall not, except with the consent in writing of the landlord and of the Commission, sub-divide his croft, and any sub-division of a croft otherwise than with such consent shall be null and void.

GENERAL NOTE

The forms to be used when applying for consent to sub-divide a croft are available from the Crofters Commission, 4/6 Castle Wynd, Inverness.

Succession to croft

Bequest of croft

10.—(1) A crofter may, by will or other testamentary writing, bequeath the tenancy of his croft to any one person; but where the power conferred by this subsection is exercised in favour of a person not being a member of the crofter's family, the bequest shall be null and void unless the Commission, on application made to them by the legatee, otherwise determine.

(2) A person to whom the tenancy of a croft is bequeathed as aforesaid (in this section referred to as "the legatee") shall, if he accepts the bequest, give notice of the bequest to the landlord within 2 months after the death of the crofter, unless he is prevented by some unavoidable cause from giving such notice within that time, and in that event he shall give such notice within a further period of 4 months. If no such notice is given in accordance with the provisions of this subsection the bequest shall become null and void.

The giving of such notice shall import acceptance of the bequest and, unless the landlord intimates objection to the Commission under subsection (3) below, the legatee shall come into the place of the deceased crofter in the croft as from the date of death of the deceased crofter, and the landlord shall notify the Commission accordingly.

(3) Where notice has been given as aforesaid to the landlord he may within one month after the giving of the notice intimate to the legatee and to the Commission that he objects to receiving the legatee as tenant of the croft and shall state the grounds of his objection.

(4) If, after affording to the legatee and to the landlord an opportunity of making representations to them, the Commission are—

(a) satisfied that the objection is reasonable, they shall declare the bequest to be null and void, and shall notify the landlord and the legatee accordingly;

(b) not so satisfied, they shall notify the landlord and the legatee to that effect, and the legatee shall thereupon come into the place of the deceased crofter in the croft as from the date of the death of the deceased crofter.

(5) If the bequest becomes null and void under this section, the right to the croft shall be treated as intestate estate of the deceased crofter in accordance with Part I of the 1964 Act.

(6) Subject to the foregoing provisions of this section, any question arising with respect to the validity or effect of the bequest shall be determined by any

court having jurisdiction to determine the validity and effect of the whole testamentary writings of the deceased crofter.

DEFINITIONS
    "member of the crofter's family": s.61(2).

GENERAL NOTE
    As only one person can succeed to the tenancy of a croft, it is sensible for a crofter to make testamentary provision. Failure to do so may have unpredictable results. The forms to be used for applying for approval of a bequest of a tenancy (subs. (1)) are available from the Crofters Commission, 4/6 Castle Wynd, Inverness. There is no prescribed form of notice for intimation of a bequest by the legatee to the landlord, but it should be in writing (see s.55(1)). The requirement on the legatee to intimate the bequest to the landlord within two months of the date of death can be extended for a further four months where he is prevented by some unavoidable cause (subs. (2)). Unfortunately "unavoidable cause" is not defined nor is it clear whether any purported delay or failure in intimation is to be dealt with as a landlord's objection (under subs. (3)).
    It should be noted that subss. (1)–(5) deal with the *right to the tenancy* and not necessarily the *value* of the deceased's interest as tenant of the croft.

Intestacy

11.—(1) Where, owing to the failure of a crofter to bequeath the tenancy of his croft or of such a bequest to receive effect, the right to the tenancy of the croft falls to be treated as intestate estate of the deceased crofter in accordance with Part I of the 1964 Act, and the tenancy is transferred in pursuance of section 16(2) of that Act, the executor of the deceased crofter shall as soon as may be furnish particulars of the transferee to the landlord, who shall accept the transferee as tenant; and the landlord shall notify the Commission accordingly.

(2) If at the expiry of a period of 3 months commencing with the relevant date the executor has not furnished to the landlord particulars of any transferee in accordance with subsection (1) above, the landlord shall forthwith notify the Commission to that effect.

(3) In this section "the relevant date" means—

(a) where the deceased crofter has exercised his power to bequeath the tenancy of the croft in favour of a person not being a member of the deceased crofter's family and the Commission, on application made to them by the legatee, have refused to determine that the bequest shall not be null and void, the date of the Commission's refusal;

(b) where the deceased crofter has otherwise failed to bequeath the tenancy, the date of death of the deceased crofter;

(c) where the deceased crofter has bequeathed the tenancy and the bequest has become null and void under section 10(2) of this Act, the date on which the bequest became null and void as aforesaid;

(d) where the deceased crofter has bequeathed the tenancy and the Commission have declared the bequest to be null and void under section 10(4) of this Act, the date on which the Commission notified the landlord and the legatee to that effect.

(4) If at the expiry of the said period of 3 months it appears to the Commission, whether from a notification under subsection (2) above or otherwise, that the executor has not furnished to the landlord particulars of any transferee in accordance with subsection (1) above, the Commission may give notice in such manner as they may think proper, whether by advertisement or otherwise, to persons who may claim to be entitled—

(a) to succeed to the intestate estate of the deceased crofter, or

(b) to claim legal rights or the prior rights of a surviving spouse out of that estate,

requiring them if they desire to have the tenancy of the croft transferred to them in or towards satisfaction of their entitlement or claim to give intimation accordingly to the Commission before such date as may be specified in the notice, being a date not earlier than 6 months after the relevant date; and the Commission may, subject to subsection (5) below, nominate as successor to the tenancy any one of the persons who have so given intimation.

(5) The Commission shall, before nominating any person as successor to the tenancy of the croft in pursuance of subsection (4) above, consult with the executor (if any) of the deceased crofter, and the Commission shall not nominate any person as successor unless it appears to them—

    (a) that that person is a person entitled to succeed to the intestate estate of the deceased crofter, or to claim legal rights or the prior rights of a surviving spouse out of that estate, and

    (b) that adequate provision is being, or will be, made for the settlement of the entitlement or claim in the said intestate estate of any other person who is known to them to be entitled to succeed to, or to claim any such rights out of, that estate.

(6) The Commission shall give notice to the landlord of any person nominated by them in pursuance of subsection (4) above, and the landlord shall accept that person as successor to the tenancy of the croft.

(7) The nomination by the Commission, in pursuance of subsection (4) above, of any person as successor to the tenancy of the croft shall transfer the interest of the tenant under that tenancy to that person, and such transfer shall be in or towards satisfaction of that person's entitlement or claim in the intestate estate of the deceased crofter.

(8) If at the expiry of one month after the end of the period referred to in section 16(3)(b) of the 1964 Act the executor has not furnished to the landlord particulars of any transferee in accordance with subsection (1) above and the Commission have not nominated any person as successor under subsection (4) above, the Commission may declare the croft to be vacant and, if they do so, shall notify the landlord accordingly.

(9) Where the Commission have under the foregoing provisions of this section nominated a person as successor to the tenancy or, as the case may be, have declared the croft to be vacant, any right of any person (other than the person so nominated) in, or in relation to, the tenancy shall be extinguished.

(10) Where a croft has been declared under subsection (8) above to be vacant, the landlord shall be liable—

    (a) if the deceased crofter was at the date of his death under any liability to the Secretary of State in respect of any loan, to pay to the Secretary of State the whole or so much of the value of the improvements on the croft as will discharge the liability of the deceased crofter, and to pay to the executor of the deceased crofter, if a claim is made in that behalf not later than 12 months after the date on which the croft was declared to be vacant, any balance of the value aforesaid;

    (b) if at the date of his death the deceased crofter was not under any such liability to the Secretary of State and a claim is made in that behalf as aforesaid, to pay to the executor of the deceased crofter the value of the improvements on the croft.

In this subsection the expression "the value of the improvements on the croft" means such sum as may be agreed, or as, failing agreement, may be determined by the Land Court, to be the sum which would have been due by the landlord by way of compensation for permanent improvements if the deceased crofter had immediately before his death renounced his tenancy.

(11) Where—

    (a) a croft has been declared under subsection (8) above to be vacant consequent on the death after 27th August 1961 of a crofter who immediately before his death was qualified as mentioned in subsection (12) below; and

    (b) the value of the improvements on the croft is determined by the Land Court under subsection (10) above, the executor of the crofter may request the Land Court to determine what would have been the value of the improvements on the croft if the Crofters (Scotland) Act 1961 had not been passed; and if the value last mentioned is greater than the value determined by the Land Court under subsection (10) above, the difference between the two said values shall be payable to the executor by the Secretary of State:

Provided that the Secretary of State shall be entitled to set off any amount due to him by the crofter at the date of his death in respect of a loan made under section 42(4) or (5) of this Act, section 22(2) or (3) of the 1955 Act or section 7(7) or 9 of the Small Landholders (Scotland) Act 1911 against any sum payable to the executor by the Secretary of State under this subsection.

(12) The reference in subsection (11) above to a crofter who immediately before his death was qualified is a reference to a crofter—

(a) whose tenancy of the croft in question began before 27th August 1961, or

(b) who held the tenancy of such croft as statutory successor to his immediate predecessor in the tenancy and each of whose predecessors (being in each case a person whose tenancy of the croft began after 27th August 1961) held such tenancy as statutory successor to his immediate predecessor.

DEFINITIONS
"member of the deceased crofter's family": s.61(2).

GENERAL NOTE
Serious difficulties may be encountered where there are several claimants equally entitled to share the estate of an intestate crofter; the deceased's interest in his croft is an item of estate much like any other. The most obvious difficulty is how to value the deceased's interest. This is required for confirmation purposes and may be subject to dispute where the value is to be divided whilst the tenancy cannot be divided. These are matters outside the Land Court's jurisdiction (see *MacLennan's Executrix* v. *MacLennan* 1974 S.L.T. (Land Ct.) 3). Where there is a demand for tenancies of crofts, the value of the deceased's interest may be considerably more than "the value of the improvements on the croft" (see subs. (1)). The executor's duty will normally be to maximise the value for the benefit of the beneficiaries entitled to share the deceased's intestate estate.

Rights of crofters and cottars to acquire their subjects

General provision

12.—(1) A crofter may, failing agreement with the landlord as to the acquisition by the crofter of croft land tenanted by him, apply to the Land Court for an order authorising him to make such acquisition.

(2) A crofter shall be entitled to a conveyance of the site of the dwelling-house on or pertaining to the croft tenanted by him, and a cottar shall be entitled to a conveyance of the site of the dwelling-house on or pertaining to his subject, and the crofter or cottar may, failing agreement with the landlord, apply to the Land Court for an order requiring the landlord to grant such a conveyance.

(3) In this Act "croft land" includes any land being part of a croft, other than—

(a) the site of the dwelling-house on or pertaining to the croft;

(b) any land, comprising any part of a common grazing, unless the land has been apportioned under section 52(4) of this Act and—

(i) is adjacent or contiguous to any other part of the croft; or

(ii) consists of arable machair;
(c) any right to mines, metals or minerals or salmon fishings (not being salmon fishings in Orkney or Shetland) pertaining to the croft.
(4) In this Act, "the site of the dwelling-house" includes any building thereon and such extent of garden ground as, failing agreement with the landlord, may be determined by the Land Court by order under 15(1) of this Act to be appropriate for the reasonable enjoyment of the dwelling-house as a residence but does not include—
(a) any right to mines, metals or minerals pertaining thereto; or
(b) where there is more than one dwelling-house on or pertaining to a croft or, as the case may be, the subject of a cottar, the site of more than one dwelling-house; or
(c) where the site of the dwelling-house on or pertaining to a croft has been acquired by the crofter after 10th June 1976, the site of any dwelling-house erected after such acquisition on or pertaining to the remainder of the croft.
(5) In this Act "cottar" means the occupier of a dwelling-house situated in the crofting counties with or without land who pays no rent, or the tenant from year to year of a dwelling-house situated as aforesaid who resides therein and who pays therefor an annual rent not exceeding £6, whether with or without garden ground but without arable or pasture land.

DEFINITIONS
    "cottar": s.12(5).
    "croft": s.3(1).
    "crofter": s.3(3).
    "landlord": s.61(1).

GENERAL NOTE
The right of a crofter to seek an owner's title to his subjects was introduced by the Crofting Reform (Scotland) Act 1976. Failing agreement with his landlord he is permitted to make an application to the Land Court.
The relevant form, the Crofter general form, is available from the Scottish Land Court, 1 Grosvenor Crescent, Edinburgh.
Separate provisions apply in respect of croft land and the site of the dwelling-house. The crofter has a qualified right to acquire croft land tenanted by him whilst he has an absolute right to a conveyance of the site of the dwelling-house on or pertaining to his croft. Should there be (or have been) more than one dwelling-house, only the site of one dwelling-house will be considered (subs. (4)(b) and (c)).
For the absolute right of purchase to apply (subs. (2)), the dwelling-house should be habitable and not be merely the ruins or remains of a former croft house. Acquisition of the site of such a building or of any second or subsequent house on the croft may be sought as part of the croft land.
Conveyance. This generally means disposition simpliciter. In *Fulton* v. *Noble* 1983 S.L.T. (Land Ct.) 40, the Land Court doubted whether feu writs were needed in crofting purchases, other than from the National Trust for Scotland (see s.16(7)).
Adjacent or contiguous. This phrase has been judicially considered. Whereas "contiguous" means "in actual contact" or "touching", "adjacent" is to be viewed more flexibly as in "close" or "neighbouring" (see *Gillies* v. *Countess of Sutherland's Trs.* 1978 S.L.T. (Land Ct.) 2).
Arable machair. There is no statutory definition of this term (s.12(3)(b)(iii)) although the meaning of the term was debated by the Scottish Standing Committee on February 5, 1976, cols. 42–50. The word "machair" has a variety of meanings in Gaelic but the term "arable machair" is particularly apt to describe the sandy coastal plains and meadowland close to the sea on the Atlantic side of the Outer Hebrides. The right of fishing for salmon in Orkney and Shetland (s.12(3)(c)) is not *inter regalia* nor does the feudal law as to salmon fishing apply in Orkney and Shetland (*Lord Advocate* v. *Balfour* 1907 S.C. 1360).
Cottar. The definition of "cottar" in subs. (5) is simply repeated from the 1955 Act, s.28(4). It should be carefully studied. Although cottars have been considered in the same legislation as crofters since 1886, there is nothing in the definition to link cottars to crofts. It appears that cottars may be found anywhere in the crofting counties, even in urban areas.

Authorisation by Land Court of acquisition of croft land

13.—(1) The Land Court, on an application made to it under section 12(1) of this Act, may make an order—

(a) authorising the crofter to acquire such croft land as may be specified in the order, subject to such terms and conditions as, failing agreement with the landlord, may be so specified, and requiring the landlord to convey the land to the crofter or his nominee in accordance with such terms and conditions; or

(b) refusing the application.

(2) The Land Court shall not make an order in accordance with subsection (1)(a) above where it is satisfied by the landlord as to either or both of the following matters—

(a) that, in all the circumstances pertaining to the landlord and having regard to the extent of land owned by him to which this Act applies, the making of such an order would cause a substantial degree of hardship to the landlord;

(b) that the making of such an order would be substantially detrimental to the interests of sound management of the estate of the landlord of which the croft land to which the application relates forms part.

(3) The Land Court, in making an order in accordance with subsection (1)(a) above, may provide that the authorisation to acquire is conditional on the crofter granting a lease to the landlord of the shooting rights over or the fishing rights pertaining to the croft land and shall so provide where it is satisfied that if such a lease were not granted the interests of the landlord in the shooting or fishing rights of which the rights being acquired by the crofter form part would be materially affected; and any such lease shall be at such nominal annual rent, for such period of not less than 20 years and subject to such other terms and conditions as the Land Court may specify.

(4) The Land Court, in making an order in accordance with subsection (1)(a) above, may include the condition that the crofter shall grant a standard security in favour of the landlord to secure any sum which may become payable to him or his personal representative under section 14(3) of this Act in the event of disposal of the croft land or any part thereof.

(5) Where the Land Court proposes to make an order authorising the crofter to acquire—

(a) land comprising any part of a common grazing which had been apportioned under subsection (4) of section 52 of this Act; or

(b) land held runrig which has been apportioned under subsection (8) of that section,

and it is satisfied that the apportionment has been made subject to conditions imposed by the Commission under subsection (6) or, as the case may be, subsection (8) of that section, it shall have regard to the conditions so imposed.

DEFINITIONS

"croft land": s.12(3).

"standard security": s.9 of the Conveyancing and Feudal Reform (Scotland) Act 1970.

GENERAL NOTE

This section relates to the qualified right of a crofter to acquire his croft land at its "crofting value". It should be read along with ss.14, 16 and 17. Although subs. (1) gives the Land Court discretion to grant or refuse an application by a crofter to purchase his croft land, in practice the result will depend on whether the landlord satisfies the Land Court that he has a valid objection.

Under subs. (2) only two possible grounds of objection are available to a landlord. The first, a plea of hardship, depends on special circumstances and any such hardship must be substantial and substantiated by evidence (*Macaskill* v. *Basil Baird & Son Ltd.* 1987 S.L.T. (Land Ct.) 34). The hardship need not be financial.

The second ground of objection requires proof that the landlord is actively engaged in estate management and that this would be affected in a substantial way (see *Geddes* v. *Martin* 1987 S.L.C.R. 104 and *Macdonald* v. *Hilleary* 1993 S.L.T. (Land Ct.) 26).

Provision is made in subs. (3) for the selling landlord to obtain a sporting lease in respect of croft land after purchase. A nominal annual rent can be as little as 10p and 21 years is a normal period, permitting the lease to be recorded in the Land Register and enforceable against singular successors (*Livingstone* v. *Nelson* 1990 S.L.C.R. 64, p.72 and *Palmers' Trustees* v. *Brown* 1989 S.L.T. 128).

It is not open to the Land Court to order a crofter acquiring his croft land to pay the landlord's legal expenses of the conveyance (*Ferguson* v. *Ross Estates Co. Ltd.* 1977 S.L.T. (Land Ct.) 19). Instead of a standard security as permitted by subs. (4), the Land Court have frequently ordered a condition to be included in the conveyance to secure any sum payable under s.14(3), in order to avoid expense.

The different position of the National Trust for Scotland as landlord is recognised in ss.16(7), 17(4) and (5).

Consideration payable in respect of acquisition of croft land

14.—(1) Where the Land Court makes an order in accordance with section 13(1)(a) of this Act and the crofter and the landlord have failed to reach agreement about the consideration payable in respect of the acquisition, the consideration shall, subject to subsection (3) below, be the crofting value of the croft land specified in the order as determined by the Land Court under subsection (2) below.

(2) The crofting value of the croft land, as determined by the Land Court for the purposes of subsection (1) above, shall be such amount as the Land Court may determine to be the proportion attributable to the croft land of the current rent payable for the croft of which the croft land forms part, such amount being multiplied by the factor of 15;

Provided that the Land Court, on an application made to it by the landlord at any time before it makes a final order under section 13(1) of this Act, may determine a fair rent for the croft which shall be deemed to be the current rent for the purposes of this subsection; and section 6(4) of this Act shall apply for the purposes of this proviso as if for the word "parties" there were substituted the words "landlord and the crofter".

(3) If the person who has acquired croft land by virtue of section 13(1) of this Act ("the former crofter") or a member of the former crofter's family who has obtained the title to that land either—

   (i) as the nominee of the former crofter, or

   (ii) from the former crofter or his nominee,

disposes of that land or any part of it ("the relevant land") to anyone who is not a member of the former crofter's family, by any means other than by a lease for crofting or agricultural purposes, forthwith or at any time within five years of the date of its acquisition by the former crofter then, subject to subsection (6) below, the person disposing of the relevant land shall pay to the landlord referred to in the said section 13(1) or to his personal representative a sum equal to one half of the difference between—

  (a) the market value of the relevant land (on the date of such disposal) which, failing agreement between the parties concerned, shall be as determined by the Land Court under subsection (4) below on the application of such landlord or personal representative; and

  (b) the consideration which was paid under subsection (1) above in respect of the relevant land.

(4) The market value of the relevant land as determined by the Land Court shall be the amount which the land, if sold in the open market by a willing seller, might be expected to realise assuming that on the date of the disposal—

(a) there were no improvements on the land which, if the land were let to a crofter, would be permanent improvements in respect of which the crofter would be entitled to compensation under section 30 of this Act on renunciation of the tenancy of the croft of which the land formed part;

(b) no other development had been carried out on the land (not being development carried out on the land, when it was subject to the tenancy of the former crofter or any of his predecessors in the tenancy, by a person other than that crofter or any of such predecessors); and

(c) no development of the land which consisted of the making of such an improvement as is referred to in paragraph (a) above were or would be permitted in pursuance of the 1972 Act.

(5) If the relevant land comprises only part of the land which was acquired under section 13(1) of this Act, the Land Court may, failing agreement between the parties concerned, on an application made to it by the person disposing of the relevant land or the landlord referred to in the said section 13(1) or his personal representative, determine for the purposes of subsection (3)(b) above the proportion of the amount of the consideration which was paid under subsection (1) above in respect of the relevant land.

(6) No payment shall be made under subsection (3) above in respect of the disposal of the relevant land in a case where payment is made in respect of such disposal in accordance with an agreement entered into between the landlord and the person disposing of that land.

DEFINITIONS
  "croft land": s.12(3).
  "member of the former crofter's family": s.61(2).
  "permanent improvement": s.30(7) and Sched. 3.

GENERAL NOTE
  Where it is left to the Land Court to fix the price of croft land, subs. (1) directs that the price is to be its "crofting value", namely 15 times the current rent of the land being purchased. Subsection (2) allows the landlord to have a new fair rent set by the Land Court before the multiplier is applied. An additional provision is that the landlord can ask for an updating of the rent at any time before the final order (see *Lawson* v. *Lord Strathcona* 1992 S.L.C.R. 67).

  The landlord who is being required to sell croft land by order of the Land Court is entitled by subs. (3) to seek a second payment or "clawback" on a subsequent disposal to anyone who is not a member of the former crofter's family. But the plain meaning of this provision has been affected by the decision of the Court of Session in *Whitbread* v. *Macdonald* 1992 S.L.T. 1144. There it was held that when the Land Court authorises acquisition under s.13(1) this is to be viewed as a single transaction and not a separate disposal of the land even where the conveyance is to a nominee outside the crofter's family. The "clawback" provision can be protected either by the acquiree granting a standard security or a condition being inserted into his conveyance (see s.13(4) and the General Note above).

Determination by Land Court of terms and conditions for conveyance of the site of the dwelling-house

15.—(1) The Land Court, on an application made to it under section 12(2) of this Act, may make an order requiring the landlord to convey the site of the dwelling-house to the crofter or cottar or his nominee with such boundaries and subject to such terms and conditions as, failing agreement, may be specified in the order.

(2) Where the parties have failed to reach agreement about the consideration payable in respect of the conveyance the consideration shall be—

(a) the amount as determined by the Land Court which the site, if sold in the open market by a willing seller, might be expected to realise assuming that—

(i) there were or would be no buildings on the site;
(ii) the site were available with vacant possession;
(iii) the site were not land to which this Act applies; and

           (iv) no development of the site were or would be permitted in pursuance of the 1972 Act;

and in addition, in a case where the landlord has provided fixed equipment on the site—

    (b) an amount equal to one half of the proportion attributable to that fixed equipment, as determined by the Land Court, of the value of the site, such value being the amount as so determined which the site, if sold as aforesaid, might be expected to realise making the assumptions referred to in sub-paragraphs (ii), (iii) and (iv) of paragraph (a) above.

(3) The Land Court in making an order under subsection (1) above may determine that any of the expenses of the conveyance of the site and other expenses necessarily incurred by the landlord in relation thereto shall be borne by the crofter or cottar;

Provided that where the order relates to the conveyance of the site of the dwelling-house on or pertaining to a croft, any such determination shall be subject to the condition that the conveyance is not included in a deed which also provides for the conveyance of croft land.

(4) Failing agreement between the parties as to the amount of such expenses, the auditor of the Land Court may, on the application of either party, determine such amount; and may determine that the expenses of taxing such expenses shall be borne by the parties in such proportion as he thinks fit.

"the site of the dwelling-house": s.12(4).

GENERAL NOTE

This section relates to the incontestable right of the crofter or cottar to acquire his house site and garden ground (s.12(2)). It should be read along with ss.16 and 17. Where a crofter is seeking to purchase his subjects he should first seek to negotiate with his landlord. Only by studying how the Land Court have dealt with purchase applications since the introduction of the crofter's right to purchase in 1976 can his strong negotiating position be fully understood. In the early 1970s there was a movement by the Government towards the abolition of the feudal system. When the Land Court came to consider what conditions were appropriate to a crofter's conveyance in terms of the 1976 Act they decided to reject the traditional conditions sought to be imposed by crofting landlords in favour of the statutory powers vested in public authorities (*Campbell* v. *Duke of Argyll Trustees* 1977 S.L.T. (Land Ct.) 22). A requirement to fence the subjects of purchase and to maintain them in a stock proof condition is normally imposed. For discussion of the consideration payable for croft house site only see *Fraser* v. *Noble* 1977 S.L.T. (Land Ct.) 8. In determining the price to be paid for fixed equipment provided by the landlord for the purpose of a sale to the crofter of the site of his dwelling-house (subs. (2)), the market value of the bare site with planning permission should be deducted from the value of the site with buildings thereon (see *Livingstone* v. *Nelson* 1990 S.L.C.R. 64).

The word "development" in subs. (2) is not to be construed by reference to s.61(1) but refers only to external improvements to the dwelling-house (see *Livingstone* v. *Nelson, supra*).

The different position of the National Trust for Scotland as landlord is recognised in ss.16(7), 17(4) and (5).

Provisions relating to conveyance

16.—(1) A landlord shall have power to execute a valid conveyance in pursuance of sections 12 to 15 of this Act, notwithstanding that he may be under any such disability as is mentioned in section 7 of the Lands Clauses Consolidation (Scotland) Act 1845.

(2) Where the Land Court is satisfied, on the application of the crofter or cottar or his nominee that the landlord has failed to execute a conveyance of land in favour of such person in compliance with an order under section 13(1) or 15(1) of this Act within such time as the Land Court considers reasonable, it shall make an order authorising its principal clerk to execute the conveyance and such other deeds as adjusted at his sight as may be necessary to give effect to the order; and a conveyance executed by the principal clerk under

this subsection shall have the like force and effect in all respects as if it had been executed by the landlord.

(3) Where the principal clerk of the Land Court has executed a conveyance in pursuance of subsection (2) above, the Land Court may make such order as it thinks fit with regard to the payment of the consideration in respect of the conveyance and in particular providing for the distribution of the sum comprised in the consideration according to the respective estates or interests of persons making claim to such sum.

(4) Notwithstanding that the Land Court has made an order under section 13(1) or 15(1) of this Act determining the terms and conditions on which land is to be conveyed, the crofter or, as the case may be, the cottar and the landlord may arrange for the conveyance of the land on any other terms and conditions that they may agree.

(5) Where a person other than the landlord is infeft in the subjects to be conveyed, the second references in sections 12(2) and 13(1) of this Act and the reference in the said section 15(1) and in the foregoing provisions of this section to the landlord shall be construed as references to the landlord and such other person for their respective rights.

(6) The Land Court in specifying in an order under the said section 13(1) or 15(1) the terms and conditions on which land is to be conveyed shall have regard to any existing land obligations as defined in section 1(2) of the Conveyancing and Feudal Reform (Scotland) Act 1970 relating to such land.

(7) Where the landlords are the National Trust for Scotland, they shall not be required to convey land by an order of the Land Court under the said section 13(1) or 15(1) otherwise than by a grant in feu; but section 4(2) of the Order confirmed by the National Trust for Scotland Order Confirmation Act 1947 (which requires the consent of the Lord Advocate to grants in feu by the Trust exceeding 8 hectares) shall not apply to such a grant.

(8) Where the Land Court is satisfied, on the application of the landlord, that the crofter or his nominee has failed to execute a standard security in favour of the landlord in compliance with a condition imposed by the Land Court under section 13(4) of this Act within such time as the Land Court considers reasonable, it shall make an order authorising its principal clerk to execute the standard security; and a standard security executed by the principal clerk under this subsection shall have the like force and effect in all respects as if it had been executed by the crofter or his nominee.

DEFINITIONS
"the National Trust for Scotland": s.61(1).
"standard security": s.9 of the Conveyancing and Feudal Reform (Scotland) Act 1970.

GENERAL NOTE
An application under subs. (2) may be made by a motion to the Land Court in the purchase application before or after the Final Order has been issued.

Provisions supplementary to sections 13 and 15

17.—(1) An order of the Land Court under section 13(1)(a) or 15(1) of this Act shall have effect for a period of 2 years from the date of intimation of the order or for such other period as may at any time be agreed to in writing by the crofter or, as the case may be, the cottar and the landlord or as may be determined by the Land Court on the application of either party.

(2) Where an order has been made by the Land Court under the said section 13(1)(a) or 15(1) in relation to croft land or the site of the dwelling-house on or pertaining to a croft or under the said section 15(1) in relation to the site of the dwelling-house on or pertaining to the subject of a cottar, then, so long as the order has effect—

  (a) the crofter shall not be entitled under section 30(1) of this Act to compensation for any permanent improvement made on the croft land or site; and

  (b) the landlord of the croft shall not be entitled under section 30(6) of this Act to recover from the crofter compensation for any deterioration of, or damage to, any fixed equipment provided by the landlord in respect of the croft land or site; or

  (c) the cottar shall not be entitled under section 36(1) of this Act to compensation for any permanent improvement made on the site,

being compensation to which the crofter and the landlord or, as the case may be, the cottar would be entitled but for this subsection.

(3) Any condition or provision to the effect that—

  (a) the superior of any feu shall be entitled to a right of pre-emption in the event of a sale thereof or any part thereof by the proprietor of the feu, or

  (b) any other person with an interest in land shall be entitled to a right of pre-emption in the event of a sale thereof or of any part thereof by the proprietor for the time being,

shall not be capable of being enforced where the sale is by a landlord to a crofter or his nominee of croft land or to a crofter or a cottar or his nominee of the site of the dwelling-house on the croft or on or pertaining to the subject of the cottar in pursuance of an order under the said section 13(1) or, as the case may be, 15(1).

(4) Where the landlords are the National Trust for Scotland, the Land Court, in making an order under the said section 13(1) or 15(1), shall have regard to the purposes of the Trust.

(5) A compulsory purchase order which authorises the compulsory purchase of land, being land which was held inalienably by the National Trust for Scotland on the date of the passing of this Act and was acquired from the Trust by a crofter in pursuance of an order under section 13(1) or 15(1) of this Act, shall in so far as it so authorises be subject to special parliamentary procedure in any case where an objection has been duly made by the Trust under the Acquisition of Land (Authorisation Procedure) (Scotland) Act 1947 and has not been withdrawn; and in this subsection "held inalienably" has the same meaning as in section 7(1) of the said Act of 1947.

(6) Where the site of the dwelling-house on or pertaining to a croft has been acquired after the passing of this Act by a person, who immediately before the acquisition was the tenant of the croft, that person and the wife or husband of that person may, so long as either of them continues to occupy the subjects conveyed, enjoy any right to cut and take peats for the use of those subjects which that person enjoyed immediately before the acquisition:

Provided that this subsection is without prejudice to any right to cut and take peats effeiring to the tenancy of the remainder of the croft.

(7) Any person acquiring croft land shall, unless and until the land ceases to be a croft by a direction of the Commission under section 24(3) of this Act, be required to give notice to the Commission of the change of ownership of the land.

DEFINITIONS

  "croft land": s.12(3).
  "the National Trust for Scotland": s.61(1).
  "the site of the dwelling-house": s.12(4).

GENERAL NOTE

  The matter of continuing peat cutting rights is clarified by the addition of the proviso in subs. (6) as recommended by the Scottish Law Commission.

Adjustment of rent for remainder of croft where part conveyed to crofter

18. Where a crofter acquires the site of the dwelling-house on or pertaining to his croft or any croft land forming part of his croft, then, notwithstanding that it is less than 7 years since the term at which the existing rent for the croft first became payable, the Land Court may, on the application of the crofter or his landlord, determine a fair rent for the part of the croft which remains subject to the tenancy of the crofter, and accordingly subsections (3) and (4) of section 6 of this Act shall apply for the purposes of such a determination as if the provisos to subsection (3) were omitted; but thereafter the said provisos shall apply to a rent so determined.

Provisions relating to existing loans and heritable securities

19.—(1) Where—

(a) a crofter who acquires the site of the dwelling-house on or pertaining to his croft is on the date of the acquisition under any liability to the Secretary of State or Highlands and Islands Enterprise ("HIE"), or

(b) a cottar who acquires the site of the dwelling-house on or pertaining to his subject is on the date of the acquisition under any liability to the Secretary of State,

in respect of any loan, the amount outstanding in respect of such liability shall be deemed, as from the last day on which the crofter or cottar was liable to pay rent in respect of that site or on which the cottar was entitled to occupy the site as a cottar, to be a loan by the Secretary of State to the crofter or cottar or, as the case may be, by HIE to the crofter, and the provisions of Schedule 5 to this Act shall apply in relation to any such loan by the Secretary of State and, subject to any necessary modifications, to any such loan by HIE.

(2) Any question arising under subsection (1) above as to the day from which the outstanding amount is deemed to be a loan shall be determined by the Land Court.

(3) Any rights of HIE created under subsection (1) above shall be postponed to any rights, whensoever constituted, of the Secretary of State under that subsection; and such rights of the Secretary of State and HIE shall have priority over any other loan in respect of which the crofter or the cottar or his nominee as owner of the site of the dwelling-house is under any liability and shall be postponed only to such items as are referred to in heads (i), (ii) and (iii) of paragraph 4(b) of Schedule 9 to the Housing (Scotland) Act 1987.

(4) Any heritable security which immediately before the execution of a conveyance in pursuance of sections 12 to 18 of this Act burdened the subjects conveyed shall, as from the date of recording of the conveyance in the Register of Sasines or of registration of the interest conveyed in the Land Register of Scotland (as the case may be)—

(a) in the case of a conveyance in feu, cease to burden the *dominium utile* of the subjects conveyed and burden only the superiority thereof;

(b) in the case of a conveyance otherwise than in feu where the heritable security burdened only the subjects conveyed, cease to burden those subjects;

(c) in the case of a conveyance otherwise than in feu where the heritable security also burdened other land, burden only that other land;

and, unless the creditors in right of any such security otherwise agree, the landlord shall pay to them according to their respective rights and preferences any sum paid to him by the crofter or cottar as consideration for the subjects conveyed.

Provisions relating to termination of tenancy and de-crofting

Resumption of croft or part of croft by landlord

20.—(1) The Land Court may, on the application of the landlord and on being satisfied that he desires to resume the croft, or part thereof, for some reasonable purpose having relation to the good of the croft or of the estate or to the public interest, authorise the resumption thereof by the landlord upon such terms and conditions as it may think fit, and may require the crofter to surrender his croft, in whole or in part, to the landlord accordingly, upon the landlord making adequate compensation to the crofter either by letting to him other land of equivalent value in the neighbourhood or by compensation in money or by way of an adjustment of rent or in such other manner as the Land Court may determine.

(2) A sum awarded as compensation under subsection (1) above shall, if the Land Court so determines, carry interest as from the date when such sum is payable at the same rate as would apply (in the absence of any such statement as is provided for in Rule 66 of the Act of Sederunt (Rules of Court, consolidation and amendment) 1965) in the case of decree or extract in an action commenced on that date in the Court of Session if interest were included in or exigible under that decree or extract.

(3) For the purposes of subsection (1) above "reasonable purpose" shall include—

  (a) the using, letting or feuing of the land proposed to be resumed for—
      (i) the building of dwellings;
      (ii) small allotments;
      (iii) harbours, piers, boat shelters or other like buildings;
      (iv) churches or other places of religious worship;
      (v) schools;
      (vi) halls or community centres;
      (vii) planting;
      (viii) roads practicable for vehicular traffic from the croft or township to the public road or to the seashore; or
      (ix) any other purpose likely to provide employment for crofters and others in the locality;
  (b) the protection of an ancient monument or other object of historical or archaeological interest from injury or destruction.

(4) Where an application is made, with the consent of a majority of the persons sharing in a common grazing and with the approval of the Commission, for authority to resume any land forming part of the common grazing for the purpose of using, letting or otherwise disposing of it for the planting of trees, the Land Court shall not withhold its authority for such resumption.

(5) Where a grazings committee have, under section 48(4) of this Act, planted trees on land forming part of a common grazing, it shall not be competent for an application to be made under subsection (1) above in respect of that land while it continues to be used as woodlands.

GENERAL NOTE

There are now two main methods of removing land from crofting controls. These are: (1) de-crofting by direction of the Crofters Commission (s.24(2) and (3)) and (2) resumption by order of the Land Court.

Where the landlord wishes to resume land tenanted by a crofter, he must apply to the Land Court. Forms are available from the Scottish Land Court, 1 Grosvenor Crescent, Edinburgh. A croft without a tenant is merely vacant and available for re-letting. Even where there is no tenant, the land still requires to be de-crofted. A sub-tenant of a croft cannot be a party to a resumption application; *Carnach Crofts Ltd.* v. *Robertson* 1973 S.L.T. (Land Ct.) 8.

The reasonable purpose must be proved to Land Court's satisfaction even if the crofter consents (see *Fennell* v. *Paterson* 1990 S.L.C.R. 42) and the fact that the purpose is listed in subs. (3) does not *ipso facto* make it a reasonable purpose (*Portman Trs* v. *MacRae* 1971 S.L.T. (Land Ct.) 6).

In 1992 the Land Court issued a Practice Note on resumption applications, which stated:

"The Court will not authorise resumption retrospectively and accordingly practitioners should ensure that applications for resumption are lodged with the Court well in advance of the date from which resumption is sought. The Court has to take account of any representations made by the crofter but in applications where all matters are agreed, the Court may authorise resumption without having a hearing.

Before authorising resumption, the Court requires to be satisfied not only that the resumption is for a reasonable purpose but also that the purpose for which resumption is sought will actually be carried out. The Court may therefore, in cases where local authority planning permission for a development is required, require evidence that this has been granted.

For the purposes of this note, resumption applications, whether from a croft or from a common grazing, can be divided into three categories:

(1) In an application where resumption is being sought of an area of ground with an existing building situated thereon for the purpose of conveying the area of ground to either the crofter respondent or a third party, the Court will not normally require any evidence of planning permission. However, the Court will wish to have evidence that the landlord and the person acquiring the area of ground in question have agreed the terms of a sale. The Court will accept as such evidence; concluded missives (conditional on resumption being granted) or an exchange of letters indicating that a sale has been agreed or indeed a statement in the application to the effect that a sale has been agreed between the landlord and the third party and the price agreed.

(2) In an application where resumption is sought of a bare land site for sale either to the crofter or to a third party for any purposes involving development under the Planning Acts (including as a site for a dwelling-house), the Court will require in addition to evidence of an agreed sale as detailed above, at least an indication that outline planning permission has been or will be granted. Normally the Court will expect to have sight of the actual grant of outline planning permission but the Court will be prepared to accept as an alternative a letter from the local authority indicating that planning permission will be granted. In the event of such an application being lodged where no planning permission has been obtained the Court will normally sist the application until such time as evidence of the grant of planning permission can be exhibited to the Court.

(3) In applications where the landlord seeks to resume ground for the purpose of conveying it to a local authority who are then to carry out work on the ground, whether it be road improvements, new drainage systems or other works, the Court will not require any evidence of planning permission but as detailed above will require evidence that the landlord had agreed to sell the area of ground in question to the local authority. In applications in this category it is common practice for the local authority to agree certain accommodation works with the crofter or crofters in question and these should be detailed either in the application form itself or by reference to appended Schedules. In such applications where accommodation works are to be carried out by the local authority or their contractors, the Court will assume that in all cases the accommodation works, unless otherwise stated, will, after satisfactory construction, become crofters' improvements and will thereafter be maintainable by them in the future. The Court's Order will normally include an obligation to carry out the accommodation works as set out in the schedule of accommodation works which is lodged along with the application or on the plan produced.

In all the above three categories the Court have indicated that evidence of an agreed sale will be required. Where, however, the crofter or crofters have executed a Minute of Consent either waiving compensation (in terms of s.20(1)) and/or the share in the development value (in terms of s.21) or have agreed to accept a certain stated amount in settlement of any claims under s.20 or s.21, it is unnecessary to indicate in the application the consideration agreed between the landlord and the third party.

It is the Court's normal practice to authorise resumption forthwith unless asked specifically in the Statement of Facts to authorise resumption at a particular date. However, there is one important exception to that practice and that is in applications where the purpose of the resumption is to convey an area of ground to a body possessing compulsory purchase powers—because in terms of the Land Compensation (Scotland) Act 1973, s.56, a crofter has the right to opt to claim compensation under the Compulsory Purchase Code instead of the

Crofting Acts. If a crofter wishes to exercise his right to opt he must do so before surrender of the ground and in order to give him time to consider whether to opt or not the Court has adopted the practice of authorising resumption and ordaining surrender at a date some four weeks later than the date of intimation of the Order so as to give the crofter time, at least in theory, to consider whether to opt or not".

Crofter's right to share in value of land resumed by landlord

21.—(1) Where the Land Court authorises the resumption of a croft or a part thereof under section 20 of this Act, the crofter shall be entitled to receive from the landlord, in addition to any compensation payable to him under that section, a share in the value of the land so resumed the amount whereof shall be one half of the difference between, subject to subsection (5) below, the market value of the land (on the date on which resumption thereof is so authorised) as determined by the Land Court in accordance with subsections (2) and (3) below (less any compensation payable as aforesaid) and the crofting value thereof.

(2) Where the resumption of the land is so authorised for some reasonable purpose which has been or is to be carried out by the landlord or by any person not being an authority possessing compulsory purchase powers, the market value for the purposes of subsection (1) above shall be a sum equal to the amount which the land, if sold in the open market by a willing seller, might be expected to realise.

(3) Where the resumption is so authorised for some reasonable purpose which has been or is to be carried out by an authority possessing compulsory purchase powers (not being the landlord) on the acquisition by them of the land so resumed, the market value for the purposes of subsection (1) above shall be a sum equal to the amount of compensation payable by the authority to the landlord in respect of the acquisition:

Provided that, where the land so resumed forms part only of the land acquired from the landlord by the authority, the market value shall be a sum equal to such amount as the Land Court may determine to be the proportion of the amount of compensation so payable by the authority which relates to the land so resumed.

(4) Where the land so resumed forms or forms part of a common grazing—

  (a) the share of the value of that land payable to the crofters sharing in the common grazing shall be apportioned among such crofters according to the proportion that the right in the common grazing of each such crofter bears to the total of such rights;

  (b) any sum so apportioned to such a crofter shall be deemed to be the share in the value of such land resumed to which he is entitled under subsection (1) above, and

  (c) the share so payable shall, if a grazings committee or a grazings constable has been appointed under section 47 of this Act, be paid by the landlord to the clerk of the committee or the constable for distribution by him among the crofters concerned:

    Provided that, if any crofter wishes the proportion of the share payable to him to be paid directly to him by the landlord, the landlord shall comply with his wishes.

(5) For the purposes of this section, where any development has been carried out by any person, other than the crofter or any of his predecessors in the tenancy, on the land which the Land Court has authorised the landlord to resume before such authorisation, there shall be deducted from the market value such amount thereof as, in the opinion of the Land Court, is attributable to that development.

(6) A sum awarded under this section shall, if the Land Court so determines, carry interest as from the date when such sum is payable at the same rate as would apply (in the absence of any such statement as is provided for in Rule 66 of the Act of Sederunt (Rules of Court, consolidation and amendment) 1965) in the case of a decree or extract in an action commenced on that

date in the Court of Session if interest were included in or exigible under that decree or extract.

(7) In this section—

"crofting value", in relation to land resumed, has the same meaning as it has in section 14 of this Act in relation to croft land;

"reasonable purpose" has the same meaning as in section 20(3) of this Act.

DEFINITIONS

"authority possessing compulsory purchase powers": s.61(1).
"development": s.61(1).

GENERAL NOTE

The 1976 Act conferred rights on crofters to share in the value of land resumed by landlords or taken possession of compulsorily. The provisions are now found in ss.21 and 37. When a croft or part thereof is resumed by the landlord under s.20, the crofter is entitled to receive, in addition to compensation under that section, a share in the value of the land so resumed. A court of five judges in the First Division of the Inner House of the Court of Session recently held that the purpose of the expression "the land so resumed" in s.21(1) was to restrict the valuation to what had been resumed by the landlord, and the crofters were not entitled to share in the mineral value of the land because the minerals did not form part of the land which had been let (*MacKenzie* v. *Barr's Trustees* 1993 S.L.T. 1228).

Care must be taken when calculating the share in the value to be paid to the crofter (subs. (1)). There are two different methods of finding the market value of the land resumed for the purpose of calculating the share payable to the crofter. These methods are set out in subss.(2) and (3). Where the land resumed is common grazing the share of the value of that land is apportioned among the crofters sharing in the common grazing. As recommended by the Scottish Law Commission, the crofters' share must be paid to them through the clerk to the grazings committee or the grazings constable, unless any particular crofter wishes to receive payment of his portion direct from the landlord. The crofter's share in the market value is not "compensation" (see *Galson Estate Ltd.* v. *Saunders* 1984 S.L.C.R. 74). It is possible to avoid a hearing on the question of valuation where parties are in agreement (see the general note to s.20).

Absentee crofters

22.—(1) If the Commission determine in relation to a croft—

(a) that the crofter is not ordinarily resident on, or within 16 kilometres of, the croft; and

(b) that it is in the general interest of the crofting community in the district in which the croft is situated that the tenancy of the crofter should be terminated and the croft let to some other person or persons;

then, subject to the provisions of this section, they shall have power to make an order terminating the tenancy of the crofter and requiring him to give up his occupation of the croft at a term of Whitsunday or Martinmas not earlier than 3 months after the making of such order.

(2) Before making an order under subsection (1) above the Commission shall take into consideration all the circumstances of the case, including the extent, if any, to which the croft is being worked and, where the croft is being worked by a member of the crofter's family, the nature of the arrangements under which it is being so worked, and shall give to the crofter and to the landlord, not less than 6 months before the term at which the proposed order will take effect, notice that they propose to make such an order and shall afford to the crofter and the landlord an opportunity of making representations to them against the making of the proposed order.

Where the Commission make such an order, they shall, not less then 3 months before the term at which the order takes effect, give notice to the crofter and to the landlord of the making of the order.

(3) Where an order has been made under subsection (1) above and the crofter has failed to give up his occupation of the croft on or before the day on

which the order takes effect, the sheriff on the application of the Commission shall, except on cause shown to the contrary, grant warrant for ejection of the crofter.

(4) The Commission may recover from the crofter the expenses incurred by them in any application under subsection (3) above and in the execution of any warrant granted thereon.

(5) A crofter shall, on the termination of his tenancy by an order made under subsection (1) above, be entitled to the like rights to, and be subject to the like liabilities in respect of, compensation as if he had renounced his tenancy at the term at which the order takes effect.

DEFINITIONS
"Martinmas": s.61(1).
"Whitsunday": s.61(1).

GENERAL NOTE
One of the principal powers exercised by the Crofters Commission over land subject to crofting controls is to make orders terminating the tenancies of absentee crofters. Such crofters as are dispossessed may be entitled to or liable for compensation (subs. (5) and ss.30 and 34).

Vacant crofts

23.—(1) Where—
(a) the landlord of a croft receives from the crofter a notice of renunciation of his tenancy or obtains from the Land Court an order for the removal of the crofter; or
(b) the landlord of the croft either gives to the executor of a deceased crofter, or receives from such an executor, notice terminating the tenancy of the croft in pursuance of section 16(3) of the 1964 Act; or
(c) for any other reason the croft has become vacant otherwise than by virtue of a declaration by the Commission in the exercise of any power conferred on them by this Act;
the landlord shall within one month from—
(i) the receipt of the notice of renunciation of the tenancy, or
(ii) the date on which the Land Court made the order, or
(iii) the date on which the landlord gave or received notice terminating the tenancy, or
(iv) the date on which the vacancy came to the landlord's knowledge,
as the case may be, give notice thereof to the Commission.

(2) Any person who, being the landlord of a croft, fails to comply with the requirements of subsection (1) above shall be guilty of an offence and shall be liable on summary conviction to a fine of an amount not exceeding level 1 on the standard scale.

(3) The landlord of a croft shall not, except with the consent in writing of the Commission, or, if the Commission withhold their consent, except with the consent of the Secretary of State, let the croft or any part thereof to any person; and any letting of the croft otherwise than with such consent shall be null and void.

(4) Where any person is in occupation of a croft under a letting which is null and void by virtue of subsection (3) above, the Commission may serve on him a notice in writing requiring him to give up his occupation of such croft on or before such day as may be specified in the notice, being a day not less than one month from the date of the service of the notice; and if he fails to give up his occupation of the croft on or before that day, subsection (3) of section 22 of this Act shall, subject to any necessary modifications, apply as it applies where a crofter fails to give up the occupation of a croft as mentioned in that subsection.

(5) Where a croft is vacant the Commission may, at any time after the expiry of one month from the occurrence of the vacancy, give notice to the landlord requiring him to submit to them his proposals for re-letting the

croft, whether as a separate croft or as an enlargement of another croft, and if, within a period of 2 months from the giving of such notice, no such proposals are submitted or such proposals are submitted but the Commission refuse to approve them, the Commission may, if they think fit, themselves let the croft to such person or persons and on such terms and conditions (including conditions as to rent) as may be fixed by the Commission after consultation with the landlord; and such let shall have effect in all respects as if it had been granted by the landlord:

Provided that the Commission shall not themselves let the croft while the Secretary of State is considering an application made to him under subsection (3) above for consent to let, or the Commission are considering an application made to them under section 24(3) of this Act for a direction that the croft shall cease to be a croft.

(6) Where a croft has been let on terms and conditions fixed by the Commission, the landlord may within one month from the date of the letting apply to the Land Court for a variation of the terms and conditions so fixed, and any variation made in pursuance of such application shall have effect as from the date of the letting.

(7) Where the Commission have under subsection (5) above let a vacant croft as an enlargement of another croft, and any of the buildings on the vacant croft thereby cease to be required in connection with the occupation of the croft, the Commission shall give notice to that effect to the landlord, and thereupon—

(a) the buildings shall cease to form part of the croft; and

(b) the landlord may, at any time within 6 months after the giving of such notice, give notice to the Secretary of State requiring him to purchase the buildings.

(8) If the landlord, within one month after the Commission issue a direction under section 24(2) of this Act that a croft shall cease to be a croft, gives notice to the Secretary of State requiring him to purchase the buildings on the croft, the Secretary of State shall purchase such buildings.

(9) Where a notice has been duly given under subsection (7)(b) or (8) above, the Secretary of State shall be deemed to be authorised to purchase the buildings compulsorily and to have served notice to treat in respect thereof on the date on which the notice aforesaid was given:

Provided that the consideration payable by the Secretary of State in respect of the purchase of the buildings shall be such sum as may be agreed by the Secretary of State and the landlord, or, failing agreement, as may be determined by the Land Court to be equal to the amount which an out-going tenant who had erected or paid for the erection of the buildings would have been entitled to receive from the landlord by way of compensation for permanent improvements in respect of the buildings as at the date on which notice was given as aforesaid to the Secretary of State requiring him to purchase the buildings.

(10) For the purposes of this section and sections 24 and 25 of this Act, a croft shall be taken to be vacant notwithstanding that it is occupied, if it is occupied otherwise than by the tenant of the croft.

(11) The provisions of this section and sections 24 and 25 of this Act shall have effect in relation to a part of a croft as they have effect in relation to a croft.

(12) This section and section 24 of this Act shall have effect as if—

(a) a person who has become the owner-occupier of a croft were required under subsection (1) above within one month of the date on which he became such owner-occupier to give notice thereof to the Commission; and

(b) any reference in this section and section 24 of this Act, other than in subsection (1) above, to a landlord included a reference to an owner-occupier.

DEFINITIONS
  "croft": s.3(1).
  "landlord": s.61.
  "notice": s.55(1).
  "removal": ss.5(2) and 26.
  "renunciation": see s.7(1).
  "vacant": subs. (10).

GENERAL NOTE
  The lack of a crofting tenant does not remove a croft from crofting controls. Resumption provisions are to be found in ss.20 and 21 and provisions relating to de-crofting in ss.24 and 25, which enable land to be released from these controls. Crofts without tenants are merely vacant and they must be notified to the Crofters Commission in writing (subs. (1)). Failure to do so renders the landlord liable to prosecution (subs. (2)). An owner-occupier is treated for this purpose as the proprietor of a vacant croft (subs. (12)) (*Cameron* v. *Bank of Scotland* 1988 S.L.C.R. 47).
  In the case of *Hastings* v. *Crofters Commission (No. 2)* 1992 S.L.T. (Land Ct.) 45 at p.50, the Land Court held that the statutory provisions relating to de-crofting were intended to apply to part of a croft although not expressly stated. The matter is made certain by subs. (11), on the recommendation of the Scottish Law Commission.

Decrofting in case of resumption or vacancy of croft

24.—(1) This Act shall cease to apply to any land on its being resumed in pursuance of an order authorising its resumption made under section 20 of this Act by the Land Court, without prejudice, however, to the subsequent exercise of any powers conferred by this Act for the enlargement of existing crofts.

(2) Where a croft has, in consequence of the making of an order under section 22(1) of this Act, become vacant and has remained unlet for a period of 6 months beginning with the date on which the croft so became vacant, the Commission shall, if the landlord at any time within 3 months after the expiry of the period aforesaid, gives notice to the Commission requiring them to do so, direct that the croft shall cease to be a croft.

(3) Where a croft is vacant, the Commission may, on the application of the landlord, direct that the croft shall cease to be a croft or refuse to grant the application; and if the Commission direct under this subsection or under sub-section (2) above that a croft shall cease to be a croft then, subject to subsection (4) below, this Act shall cease to apply to the croft, without prejudice, however, to the subsequent exercise of any powers conferred by this Act or any other enactment for the enlargement of existing crofts.

(4) The coming into effect of a direction given by the Commission by virtue of section 25(4) of this Act shall not affect the powers contained in the proviso to section 29(3) of this Act.

DEFINITIONS
  "croft": s.3.
  "enlargement": s.4.
  "notice": s.55(1).
  "vacant": s.23(10).

GENERAL NOTE
  The forms for applying for de-crofting directions (subs. (3)) are available from the Crofters Commission, 4/6 Castle Wynd, Inverness. The position of a sub-tenant is protected to a limited extent (subs. (4)). The provisions of s.24 also apply to part crofts (s.23(11)).

Provisions supplementary to s.24(3)

25.—(1) The Commission shall give a direction under section 24(3) of this Act that a croft shall cease to be a croft if—
  (a) subject to subsection (2) below, they are satisfied that the applicant has applied for the direction in order that the croft may be used for or in connection with some reasonable purpose (within the meaning of

section 20 of this Act) having relation to the good of the croft or of the estate or to the public interest and that the extent of the land to which the application relates is not excessive in relation to that purpose; or

(b) the application is made in respect of a part of a croft, which consists only of the site of the dwelling-house on or pertaining to the croft and in respect of which a crofter is entitled at the time of the application, or has been entitled, to a conveyance by virtue of section 12(2) of this Act, and they are satisfied that the extent of garden ground included in that part is appropriate for the reasonable enjoyment of the dwelling-house as a residence.

(2) Without prejudice to subsection (1)(b) above, the Commission, in determining whether or not to give such a direction, shall have regard to the general interest of the crofting community in the district in which the croft is situated and in particular to the demand, if any, for a tenancy of the croft from persons who might reasonably be expected to obtain that tenancy if the croft were offered for letting on the open market on the date when they are considering the application.

(3) Where the Commission give such a direction on being satisfied as mentioned in subsection (1)(a) above, they may in the direction impose such conditions as appear to them requisite for securing that the land to which the direction relates is used for the proposed use; and if at any time they are satisfied that there has been a breach of any such condition, they may make a further direction that the land in respect of which there has been such a breach shall be a vacant croft.

(4) The Commission may, on the application of a crofter who is proposing to acquire croft land or the site of the dwelling-house on or pertaining to his croft, give a direction under the said section 24(3) as if the land were a vacant croft and the application were made by the landlord, that in the event of such acquisition of the land it shall cease to be a croft, or refuse the application; but such a direction shall not have effect until the land to which it relates has been acquired by the crofter or his nominee and unless the acquisition is made within 5 years of the date of the giving of the direction.

(5) A direction under the said section 24(3) may be given taking account of such modification of the application in relation to which the direction is given as the Commission consider appropriate.

(6) The Commission shall advertise all applications under the said section 24(3) or subsection (4) above (except an application made in respect of a part of a croft consisting only of the site of the dwelling-house on or pertaining to the croft) in one or more newspapers circulating in the district in which the croft to which the application relates is situated, and before disposing of such an application shall, if requested by the applicant, afford a hearing to the applicant and to such other person as they think fit.

(7) The Commission shall give notice in writing to the applicant of their proposed decision on an application made to them under the said section 24(3) or subsection (4) above, specifying the nature of and the reasons for such decision.

(8) The applicant may within 21 days of receipt of the notice under subsection (7) above, and the owner of land to which a further direction under subsection (3) above relates may within 21 days of the making of that further direction, appeal against the proposed decision or further direction to the Land Court who may hear or consider such evidence as it thinks fit in order to enable it to dispose of the appeal.

(9) The Commission shall give effect to the determination of the Land Court on an appeal under subsection (8) above.

DEFINITIONS
"croft land": s.12(3).
"site of the dwelling-house": s.12(4).
"vacant": s.23(10).

GENERAL NOTE

The forms for applying for de-crofting directions (ss.24(3) and 25(4)) are available from the Crofters Commission, 4/6 Castle Wynd, Inverness.

The area comprising the site of the dwelling house will be identified and de-crofted on the same basis as the Land Court would require the landlord to grant a conveyance thereof to the crofter (subs. (1)(b)). A shortened procedure is prescribed (subs. (6)).

A croft (or part thereof; see s.23(11)) will be de-crofted for a "reasonable purpose" such as would permit the Land Court to authorise its resumption (subs. (1)(a)). However the Crofters Commission must take account of the general interest of the crofting community as well as the demand for crofting land (subs. (2)).

A de-crofting direction should be scrutinized to see if any conditions have been imposed. A breach thereof might result in the land being returned to crofting controls (subs. (3)). De-crofting can be sought by a crofter proposing to acquire his subjects but any direction obtained by him will fall if the acquisition is not completed within five years (subs. (4)).

There is a right of appeal to the Land Court where the Crofters Commission can be a party (*Hastings* v. *Crofters Commission* 1992 S.L.T. (Land Ct.) 15).

Provisions as to removal of crofter

26.—(1) When—

(a) one year's rent of a croft is unpaid, or

(b) a crofter has broken one or more of the statutory conditions (other than the condition as to payment of rent),

the Land Court may, on the application of the landlord and after considering any objections stated by the crofter, make an order for the removal of the crofter.

(2) When a crofter whose rights to compensation for permanent improvements have been transferred in whole or in part to the Secretary of State under section 43 of this Act—

(a) has abandoned his croft; or

(b) has broken any of the statutory conditions (other than the condition as to payment of rent); or

(c) has broken any of the conditions of repayment of a loan contained in the agreement for the loan;

the Land Court may, on the application of the Secretary of State and after considering any objections stated by the crofter or the landlord, make an order for the removal of the crofter.

(3) If a crofter is removed from his croft, the landlord shall be entitled to set off all rent due or to become due against any sum found to be due by the landlord to the crofter or to the Secretary of State for permanent improvements made on the croft.

DEFINITIONS

"compensation for permanent improvements": s.30.

"loan": ss.42 and 43.

"permanent improvements": Sched. 3.

"statutory conditions": Sched. 2.

GENERAL NOTE

Where a breach of the statutory conditions is capable of being remedied, the Land Court will allow the defaulting tenant an opportunity of remedying the breach (see, *e.g. Corbett* v. *MacLeod* 1990 S.L.C.R. 25).

The application forms are available from the Scottish Land Court, 1 Grosvenor Square, Edinburgh.

Subletting of crofts

Provisions as to right to sublet

27.—(1) Notwithstanding any enactment or rule of law, a crofter shall be entitled to sublet his croft without the consent of the landlord of the croft.

(2) A crofter shall not sublet his croft otherwise than with the consent in writing of the Commission and in accordance with such conditions (which shall not include conditions relating to rent) as the Commission in giving their consent may impose; and any sublease of his croft granted by a crofter otherwise than as aforesaid shall be null and void:

Provided that nothing in this subsection shall be construed as debarring a crofter from subletting any dwelling-house or other building forming part of his croft to holiday visitors.

(3) On applying to the Commission for their consent to a proposed sublease of his croft, a crofter shall furnish such information with respect to the proposed sublease, including the name of the subtenant, the duration of the sublease and the terms and conditions of the sublease (other than those relating to rent), as the Commission may require.

(4) The Commission shall, on an application being made to them by a crofter for their consent to a proposed sublease of a croft, serve on the landlord of the croft a notice stating that such application has been made and specifying the name and designation of the proposed subtenant, and in deciding whether to give or to refuse consent to such sublease the Commission shall have regard to any observations made to them by the landlord within 14 days commencing with the date of the service of such notice.

(5) The Commission may, in giving their consent to a proposed sublease of a croft, impose such conditions (other than any relating to rent) as they may think fit.

GENERAL NOTE

Application forms are available from the Crofters Commission, 4/6 Castle Wynd, Inverness.

For miscellaneous provisions regarding sub-leases of crofts, see s.29. The position of a subtenant can be protected to a limited extent when de-crofting has been granted (s.24(4)) or where the tenancy of a croft is brought to an end (s.29(3)).

Special provisions regarding subletting of crofts not adequately used

28.—(1) Where the Commission are of the opinion that any crofter is failing to make adequate use of his croft, they may serve on him a preliminary notice setting out their opinion as aforesaid and stating that, unless he satisfies them within one year from the date of the service of such preliminary notice that he is making adequate use of his croft, the Commission may, in accordance with subsection (2) below, serve on him a notice of requirement to sublet.

The Commission may at any time withdraw a preliminary notice served by them on a crofter under this subsection.

(2) Where a crofter on whom a preliminary notice has been served under subsection (1) above fails to satisfy the Commission within the period mentioned in that subsection that he is making adequate use of his croft, the Commission may, within 1 month from the expiry of that period, serve on such crofter a notice stating that, subject to subsection (3) below, the croft will, on the expiry of 1 month from the date of the service of the notice or such longer period as may be specified in the notice, become subject to a requirement that it be sublet.

(3) A crofter on whom a notice is served under subsection (2) above by the Commission may, at any time before his croft becomes subject, in terms of such notice, to a requirement that it be sublet, refer to the Secretary of State the question whether he is making adequate use of his croft, and the Secretary of State, after affording to the crofter an opportunity of making representations to him and, if the crofter does not object to such consultation, after consulting with any grazings committee appointed under section 47 of this Act in respect of common grazings in the township in which the croft is situated, may annul the notice or may confirm it.

(4) Where a notice is served under subsection (2) above on a crofter by the Commission and either no reference is made under subsection (3) above to the Secretary of State by the crofter or on such a reference the Secretary of State confirms the notice, the Commission may, within 1 month from the last date on which a reference might have been made as aforesaid or from the date on which the notice was confirmed by the Secretary of State, as the case may be, serve on the crofter a further notice requiring that he shall, within 3 months from the date of the service of such further notice, submit to them for their approval proposals (other than any relating to rent) for subletting his croft.

(5) The Commission shall, on proposals for subletting a croft being submitted to them by a crofter as aforesaid, serve on the landlord of the croft a notice stating that such proposals have been submitted and specifying the name and designation of the proposed subtenant, and in deciding whether or not to approve such proposals the Commission shall have regard to any observations made to them by the landlord within 14 days from the date of the service of such notice.

(6) The Commission may, in giving their approval to any proposals submitted to them by a crofter as aforesaid, impose such conditions (other than any relating to rent) as they may think fit, and any reference in this section or in section 29 of this Act to proposals submitted to the Commission under subsection (4) above and approved by them shall include a reference to conditions imposed by the Commission under this subsection in giving their approval to such proposals.

(7) If a crofter on whom a further notice is served under subsection (4) above by the Commission fails within the period mentioned in that subsection to submit proposals for subletting his croft, or if any proposals submitted by such a crofter are not approved by the Commission, or if such a crofter fails to sublet the croft in accordance with proposals approved by the Commission, the Commission themselves may, subject to the following provisions of this section, grant a sublease of the croft to such person as they may think fit.

(8) Before granting a sublease of any croft under subsection (7) above the Commission shall consult with any grazings committee appointed under section 47 of this Act in respect of common grazings in the township in which the croft is situated, and thereafter the Commission shall, if they propose to grant such sublease, serve on the landlord of the croft and on the crofter a notice to that effect which shall also specify the name and designation of the proposed subtenant, and in deciding whether or not to grant the sublease the Commission shall have regard to any observations made to them by the landlord or by the crofter within 14 days from the date of the service of such notice.

(9) Where the Commission grant a sublease of any croft under subsection (7) above, they shall forthwith give to the landlord of the croft, to the crofter and to the subtenant under the sublease a notice intimating that they have granted the sublease as aforesaid and setting out the name of the subtenant, the duration of the sublease, and the terms and conditions on which it has been granted, and the Commission shall also make a record of the condition as at the date of entry under the sublease of any fixed equipment let thereunder.

(10) A sublease of a croft granted by the crofter in accordance with proposals submitted to the Commission under subsection (4) above and approved by them, or by the Commission under subsection (7) above, shall not, unless the crofter so wishes, include the sublease of—

(a) any dwelling-house or garden ground forming part of the croft;
(b) any buildings or other structures erected, or any works executed, on the croft which, by virtue of subsection (2) or (3) of section 31 of this Act, are permanent improvements on the croft;

(c) such part of the croft as the Commission shall determine, being a part which (taken together with the site of any dwelling-house, garden ground, buildings, structures or works which, by virtue of the foregoing provisions of this subsection, are not included in the sublease) extends to one half hectare;

(d) any right pertaining to the tenancy of the croft to cut or take peat.

(11) A sublease of any croft granted under subsection (7) above by the Commission shall have effect in all respects as if it has been granted by the crofter in accordance with proposals submitted to the Commission under subsection (4) above and approved by them.

(12) The rent payable under a sublease granted under subsection (7) above by the Commission shall, in the case of a sublease of a whole croft, or of a whole croft other than any subjects which, by virtue of subsection (10) above, are not included in the sublease, be a sum equal to one and one quarter times the rent payable to the landlord by the crofter in respect of the croft, and, in any other case, be such proportion of the said sum as the Commission may determine:

Provided that the Land Court may, on an application in that behalf made by the crofter within 6 months from the date on which notice intimating the grant of the sublease was given to him under subsection (9) above by the Commission, vary the rent fixed by or under this subsection and substitute therefor such other rent, whether higher or lower than the rent so fixed, as may appear to the Land Court to be just in all the circumstances, and the rent determined by the Land Court in pursuance of this proviso shall be payable under the sublease, in place of the rent fixed as aforesaid, as from the date of entry under the sublease.

(13) The duration of any sublease granted under subsection (7) above by the Commission shall, subject to subsection (14) below and section 29(3) of this Act, be such number of years, not exceeding 5, as the Commission may determine, and any such sublease shall be granted subject to the following terms and conditions—

(a) the subtenant shall make adequate use of the land comprised in the sublease;

(b) the subtenant shall maintain any permanent improvements existing on such land at the date of the commencement of the sublease in as good a state of repair as they were in at the said date and, if he fails to do so, shall on the termination of the sublease pay to the crofter the cost, as at the date of such termination, of making good any deterioration of, or damage to, such improvements due to his failure, which cost shall, failing agreement between the subtenant and the crofter, be determined by the Land Court;

(c) the subtenant shall not make any permanent improvements on the land comprised in the sublease, other than an improvement falling under head 3, 4, 5 or 6 of Schedule 3 to this Act, and the crofter shall not be held responsible for the maintenance of any permanent improvements erected by the subtenant without the consent of the crofter;

and to such other terms and conditions as may be specified in the sublease.

(14) If the Commission are satisfied in relation to any sublease granted by them under subsection (7) above—

(a) that the subtenant has broken one or more of the terms or conditions of the sublease, or

(b) where representations in that behalf are made by the crofter or by the subtenant, that the circumstances of either of them have so materially altered that it is reasonable that the sublease should be terminated,

the Commission may serve on the crofter and on the subtenant a notice in writing terminating the sublease on such date as may be specified in the notice, being a date not later than one year from the date of the service of the notice.

(15) Where any person occupying a croft—

(a) has, by virtue of any of the provisions of this section, ceased to be entitled to occupy such croft; or

(b) is a subtenant to whom the croft has been sublet by the crofter after the date on which a further notice was served on the crofter by the Commission under subsection (4) above and otherwise than in accordance with proposals submitted to the Commission under that subsection and approved by them;

the Commission may serve on such person a notice in writing requiring him to give up his occupation of the croft on or before such date as may be specified in the notice, being a date not less than one month from the date of the service of the notice; and if he fails to give up his occupation of the croft on or before the date so specified, section 22(3) of this Act shall, subject to any necessary modifications, apply as it applies where a crofter fails to give up the occupation of a croft as mentioned in that subsection.

(16) In this section "adequate use" in relation to a croft means such use of the croft for agriculture as, having regard to its nature and location, a tenant reasonably skilled in husbandry might be expected to make of it.

(17) This section shall come into operation on a day appointed by the Secretary of State by order made by statutory instrument, but no order shall be made under this subsection unless a draft of such order has been laid before Parliament and approved by resolution of each House thereof.

GENERAL NOTE

The special provisions now contained in s.28 first appeared in the Crofters (Scotland) Act 1961 (as s.12), but have not yet been brought into operation. Subsection (17) indicates that a Statutory Instrument is still required.

Miscellaneous provisions regarding subleases of crofts

29.—(1) Subject to subsection (2) below, the subtenant under a sublease of a croft shall not be held to be a crofter or to be the tenant of an agricultural holding within the meaning of the Agricultural Holdings (Scotland) Act 1991.

(2) Where under a sublease of any croft a right in any common grazing is let to the subtenant, and the sublease is one which—

(a) has been intimated to the Commission under section 11(1)(a) or (b) of the Crofters (Scotland) Act 1961; or

(b) has been granted by the crofter with the consent of the Commission and in accordance with any conditions imposed by them, as mentioned in section 27(2) of this Act, or

(c) has been granted by the crofter in accordance with proposals submitted to the Commission under section 28(4) of this Act and approved by them, or

(d) has been granted under section 28(7) of this Act by the Commission, the subtenant shall come in place of the crofter in relation to any matter which concerns such right, and any grazings regulations applicable to such common grazing shall apply to the subtenant accordingly.

(3) Where the tenancy of a croft is terminated, any sublease of that croft subsisting immediately before the date of such termination shall come to an end on that date:

Provided that where a sublease comes to an end by virtue of the foregoing provisions of this subsection the Commission may, on an application in that behalf made to them by the subtenant within one month or such longer period not exceeding 3 months as the Commission may in all the circumstances think reasonable from the date on which the sublease came to an end as aforesaid, make an order permitting the subtenant to remain in occupation of the croft for such period, not exceeding one year from the said date, and subject to such conditions, as may be specified in the order; and no proceedings for the removal of the subtenant from the croft shall be taken by the owner of the croft before the expiry of the said period of one month or the said longer period or, if an application is made under this subsection to the Commission by the subtenant within that period, before the date of the determination of the Commission on such application.

(4) In this section and in sections 27 and 28 of this Act any reference to a croft shall include a reference to a part of a croft.

<small>GENERAL NOTE</small>

The principal provisions regarding sub-leases are contained in s.27. A limited protection is available to a sub-tenant where the tenancy of a croft is brought to an end (subs. (3)).

Compensation for improvements and for deterioration or damage

Compensation to crofter for improvements

30.—(1) Where—

(i) a crofter renounces his tenancy or is removed from his croft, or

(ii) the tenancy of a croft, being a tenancy the interest of the tenant under which is comprised in the estate of a deceased crofter, is terminated in pursuance of section 16(3) of the 1964 Act,

the crofter or, as the case may be, the executor of the deceased crofter shall, subject to the provisions of this Act, be entitled to compensation for any permanent improvement made on the croft if—

(a) the improvement is suitable to the croft; and

(b) the improvement was executed or paid for by the crofter or, as the case may be, the deceased crofter, or any of the predecessors of the crofter or of the deceased crofter in the tenancy; and

(c) either the improvement was executed otherwise than in pursuance of a specific agreement in writing under which the crofter or, as the case may be, the deceased crofter was bound to execute the improvement or, if the improvement was executed in pursuance of such an agreement, the crofter has not received or, as the case may be, the decreased crofter did not receive and his executor has not received, by way of reduction of rent or otherwise, fair consideration for the improvement.

(2) Where—

(a) a person on becoming the tenant of a croft has with the consent of the landlord paid to the outgoing tenant any compensation due to him in respect of any permanent improvement and has agreed with the Secretary of State to assume any outstanding liability to the Secretary of State of the outgoing tenant in respect of any loan made to him; or

(b) on a person becoming the tenant of a croft the Secretary of State on his behalf has paid to the landlord a sum representing the value to such person of an existing improvement on the croft,

such person shall for the purposes of subsection (1) above be deemed to have executed or paid for the improvement.

For the purposes of paragraph (a) above, a landlord who has not paid the compensation due either to the outgoing tenant or to the Secretary of State and has not applied to the Secretary of State to determine under subsection (4) of section 43 of this Act that any amount due by him to the Secretary of State by virtue of subsection (3) of that section shall be deemed to be a loan by the Secretary of State to him shall be deemed to have given his consent.

(3) Subsection (1) above shall not apply to any buildings erected by a crofter in contravention of any interdict or other judicial order.

(4) The amount of the compensation payable under subsection (1) above shall, failing agreement, be fixed by the Land Court.

(5) Nothing in this Act shall affect the provisions of the Agricultural Holdings (Scotland) Act 1991 with respect to the payment to outgoing tenants of compensation for improvements:

Provided that—

(a) where any improvements are valued under that Act with a view to the payment of compensation to a crofter or to the executor of a deceased crofter, the valuation shall, unless the landlord and the crofter or executor otherwise agree in writing, be made by the Land Court; and

(b) compensation shall not be payable under that Act for an improvement for which compensation is payable under this Act.

(6) Notwithstanding anything in this section—

(a) a crofter who immediately before 1st October 1955 was a statutory small tenant, or

(b) the statutory successor of such a crofter, or

(c) the executor of such a crofter or of such a statutory successor,

shall not be entitled, in respect of any permanent improvement made or begun before 1st October 1955, to any compensation to which he would not have been entitled if his tenancy had expired immediately before 1st October 1955.

(7) In this Act "permanent improvement" means any of the improvements specified in Schedule 3 to this Act:

Provided that no building or other structure erected on a croft shall be held to be a permanent improvement on the croft unless it is a fixture on the land.

DEFINITIONS

"removed": ss.5(2) and 26.
"renounces": s.7(1).

GENERAL NOTE

The assessment of compensation for permanent improvements is dealt with in s.32.

The forms for applying to have compensation assessed are available from the Scottish Land Court, 1 Grosvenor Crescent, Edinburgh (see subs. (4)).

Permanent improvements made on crofts for purposes of subsidiary or auxiliary occupations

31.—(1) A crofter may erect any buildings or other structures, or execute any works, on his croft which—

(a) are reasonably required to enable him to make use of the croft for any subsidiary or auxiliary occupation in accordance with paragraph 3 of Schedule 2 to this Act, and

(b) will not interfere substantially with the use of the croft as an agricultural subject.

(2) Any buildings or other structures erected, or any works executed, under subsection (1) above on any croft shall, if in the case of any such buildings or structures they are fixtures on the land, be permanent improvements on the croft and shall be deemed to be suitable to the croft for the purposes of section 30(1)(a) of this Act.

(3) The provisions of subsection (2) above shall apply in relation to buildings or other structures erected, or works executed, on any croft before 27th August 1961 if such buildings, structures or works could have been erected or executed under subsection (1) above if the said subsection (1) had then been in force:

Provided that nothing in this subsection shall authorise the payment of compensation under section 14 of the 1955 Act in respect of any such buildings, structures or works as are mentioned in this subsection where the crofter has renounced his tenancy or has been removed from his croft before 27th August 1961.

Assessment of compensation for improvements

32.—(1) The amount of any compensation payable under section 30(1) of this Act to a crofter who renounces his tenancy or is removed from his croft, or to the executor of a deceased crofter, in respect of a permanent improvement on the croft shall be a sum equal to—
  (a) the value of that improvement as at the date when—
            (i) the crofter renounced his tenancy, or
            (ii) the crofter was removed from the croft, or
            (iii) the tenancy of the croft was terminated in pursuance of section 16(3) of the 1964 Act,
      as the case may be, calculated in accordance with subsection (2) below, less
  (b) the value of any assistance or consideration which may be proved to have been given by the landlord of the croft or any of his predecessors in title in respect of the improvement.

(2) For the purposes of subsection (1) above, the value of an improvement on any croft shall be taken to be the amount, if any, which, having regard to the location of the croft and any other circumstances which might affect the demand for the tenancy thereof, the landlord might reasonably be expected to receive in respect of the improvement from a person who might reasonably be expected to obtain the tenancy of the croft if the croft were offered on the open market for letting with entry on the date referred to in subsection (1)(a) above.

(3) Where—
  (a) compensation falls to be assessed under subsections (1) and (2) above in respect of any permanent improvement on a croft; and
  (b) the amount of such compensation is fixed or assessed by the Land Court under section 30(4) or 39(3)(a) of this Act,
then, if the crofter, or (as the case may be) the executor of the deceased crofter, is qualified as mentioned in subsection (4) below, he may request the Land Court to determine the amount which would have been payable by way of compensation in respect of that improvement if the Crofters (Scotland) Act 1961 had not been passed; and if the amount last mentioned is greater than the amount fixed or assessed by the Land Court as aforesaid, the difference between the two said amounts shall be payable to the crofter or executor by the Secretary of State:
  Provided that—
  (a) the Secretary of State shall be entitled to set off any amount due to him by the crofter or, as the case may be, the executor of the deceased crofter in respect of a loan made under section 22(2) or (3) of the 1955 Act, section 42(4) or (5) of this Act or section 7(7) or section 9 of the Small Landholders (Scotland) Act 1911 against any sum payable to the crofter or executor by the Secretary of State under this subsection; and
  (b) this subsection shall not apply where compensation in respect of the improvement in question has on a previous occasion fallen to be assessed under subsections (1) and (2) above.

(4) The reference in subsection (3) above to a crofter who is qualified is a reference to a crofter—
  (a) whose tenancy of the croft in question began before 27th August 1961, or
  (b) who holds the tenancy of such croft as statutory successor to his immediate predecessor in the tenancy and each of whose predecessors

(being in each case a person whose tenancy of the croft began on or after 27th August 1961) held such tenancy as statutory successor to his immediate predecessor,

and for the purposes of the said subsection the executor of a deceased crofter shall be deemed to be qualified if the deceased crofter would have been qualified as mentioned in the foregoing provisions of this subsection.

Record of improvements

33.—(1) The Land Court shall, on the application of the landlord or the crofter, make a record of the condition of the cultivation of a croft and of the buildings and other permanent improvements thereon, and by whom the permanent improvements have been executed or paid for.

(2) Any application under this section shall be intimated by the Land Court to the other party concerned and each party shall be given an opportunity of being heard on any matter affecting the record of the croft.

DEFINITIONS
  "croft": s.3(1).
  "crofter": s.3(3).
  "landlord": s.61.
  "permanent improvements": s.30(7) and Sched. 3.

GENERAL NOTE
  Application forms are available from the Scottish Land Court, 1 Grosvenor Crescent, Edinburgh.

Compensation to landlord for deterioration or damage

34.—(1) Where—
  (a) a crofter renounces his tenancy or is removed from his croft, or
  (b) the tenancy of a croft, being a tenancy the interest of the tenant under which is comprised in the estate of a deceased crofter, is terminated in pursuance of section 16(3) of the 1964 Act,
the landlord shall be entitled to recover from the crofter or, as the case may be, from the executor of the deceased crofter compensation for any deterioration of, or damage to, any fixed equipment provided by the landlord committed or permitted by the crofter or, as the case may be, by the deceased crofter or his executor.

(2) The amount of the compensation payable under subsection (1) above shall be the cost, as at the date of the crofter's quitting the croft or, as the case may be, of the termination of the tenancy, of making good the deterioration or damage; and the landlord shall be entitled to set off the amount so payable against any compensation payable by him in respect of permanent improvements.

(3) The amount of the compensation payable under subsection (1) above shall, failing agreement, be fixed by the Land Court.

DEFINITIONS
  "removed": ss.5(2) and 26.
  "renounces": s.7(1).

GENERAL NOTE
  The forms for applying to have compensation for deterioration or damage assessed are available from the Scottish Land Court, 1 Grosvenor Crescent, Edinburgh.

Assessment of compensation for improvements or deterioration on joint application to Land Court

35. Where—
  (a) a crofter has given notice of renunciation of his tenancy, or

(b) the landlord of the croft either gives to the executor of a deceased crofter, or receives from such an executor, notice terminating the tenancy of the croft in pursuance of section 16(3) of the 1964 Act,

the Land Court may, on the joint application of the crofter or, as the case may be, the executor of the deceased crofter and the landlord or, where the crofter's rights to compensation for permanent improvements have been transferred in whole or in part under section 43 of this Act to the Secretary of State, on the joint application of the Secretary of State and the landlord, assess prior to the renunciation or, as the case may be, the termination the amounts which will on renunciation or termination become due under sections 30 and 34 of this Act by the landlord by way of compensation for permanent improvements and by the crofter or executor by way of compensation for deterioration or damage; and the amounts so assessed shall, on renunciation or, as the case may be, termination, become due accordingly.

DEFINITIONS
  "renunciation": s.7(1).
  "termination": ss.20 and 22.

GENERAL NOTE
  Application forms are available from the Scottish Land Court, 1 Grosvenor Crescent, Edinburgh.

Compensation to cottar for improvements

36.—(1) Where a cottar if not paying rent is removed from his dwelling and any land or buildings occupied by him in connection therewith, or if paying rent renounces his tenancy or is removed, he shall be entitled to compensation for any permanent improvement if—
  (a) the improvement is suitable to the subject; and
  (b) the improvement was executed or paid for by the cottar or the cottar's wife or husband or any predecessor of the cottar or of the cottar's wife or husband; and
  (c) either the improvement was executed otherwise than in pursuance of a specific agreement in writing under which the cottar was bound to execute the improvement, or, if the improvement was executed in pursuance of such an agreement, the cottar has not received, by way of reduction of rent or otherwise, fair consideration for the improvement.

(2) The amount of the compensation payable under subsection (1) above shall, failing agreement, be fixed by the Land Court, and sections 30(3) and 32(1) and (2) of this Act shall apply in relation to such cottar as they apply in relation to crofters.

(3) Where the amount of the compensation payable under subsection (1) above is fixed by the Land Court under subsection (2) above, then, if the cottar is qualified as mentioned in subsection (4) below, he may request the Land Court to determine the amount which would have been payable by way of compensation in respect of the permanent improvement concerned if the Crofters (Scotland) Act 1961 had not been passed; and if the amount last mentioned is greater than the amount fixed by the Land Court as aforesaid, the difference between the two said amounts shall be payable to the cottar by the Secretary of State:

Provided that—
  (a) the Secretary of State shall be entitled to set off any amount due to him by the cottar in respect of a loan made under section 22(2) of the 1955 Act, section 42(4) of this Act or section 9 of the Small Landholders

(Scotland) Act 1911 against any sum payable to the cottar by the Secretary of State under this subsection; and

(b) this subsection shall not apply where compensation in respect of the improvement in question has on a previous occasion fallen to be assessed under section 32(1) and (2) of this Act as applied by subsection (2) above.

(4) The reference in subsection (3) above to a cottar who is qualified is a reference to a cottar—

(a) whose occupation of the subject in question began before 27th August 1961; or

(b) who occupies such subject as heir-at-law, legatee or assignee of his immediate predecessor as occupier of the subject, and each of whose predecessors (being in each case a person whose occupation of the subject began on or after 27th August 1961) occupied the subject as heir-at-law, legatee or assignee of his immediate predecessor.

(5) In this section "predecessor", in relation to a cottar or to the wife or husband of a cottar, means any person to whom the cottar or the wife or husband of the cottar might, failing nearer heirs, have succeeded in case of intestacy.

GENERAL NOTE

Although cottars have had statutory status since the 1886 Act, subsequent legislation has made little additional provision for them.

It should be remembered that there is no right of succession to a cottar's subjects. Nor has the executor of a deceased cottar any claim against either the landowner or former landlord. Any person occupying a cottar's subjects, following the death of a cottar, must have the agreement of the landowner or landlord, which agreement may be withheld.

Given the risk of loss of his subjects, a cottar would be well advised to seek an owner's title to his subjects without delay (see s.12(2)).

Compulsory acquisition of croft

Crofter's right to share in value of land taken possession of compulsorily

37.—(1) Where in pursuance of any enactment providing for the acquisition and taking of possession of land compulsorily by any person (in this section referred to as an "acquiring authority"), an acquiring authority acquire and take possession of a croft or a part thereof from a crofter, the crofter shall be entitled to receive from the acquiring authority, in addition to any compensation payable to him under section 114 of the Lands Clauses Consolidation (Scotland) Act 1845, a share in the value of the land of which possession has been taken, the amount whereof shall be one half of the difference between, subject to subsection (4) below, the market value of the land (on the date on which such possession is taken) as determined by the Land Court in accordance with subsection (2) below (less any compensation payable as aforesaid) and the crofting value thereof.

(2) The market value for the purposes of subsection (1) above shall be a sum equal to the amount which the land, if sold in the open market by a willing seller, might be expected to realise assuming that the land were not land to which this Act applies.

(3) Section 21(4) of this Act shall apply to land which has been taken possession of compulsorily by an acquiring authority as it applies to land of which the Land Court has authorised resumption.

(4) For the purposes of this section, where any development has been carried out by any person, other than the crofter or any of his predecessors in the tenancy, on the land referred to in subsection (1) above before the land has

been acquired by and taken possession of by the acquiring authority, there shall be deducted from the market value such amount thereof as, in the opinion of the Land Court, is attributable to that development.

(5) In this section "crofting value", in relation to land which has been taken possession of compulsorily, has the same meaning as it has in section 14 of this Act in relation to croft land.

Reorganisation schemes

Reorganisation schemes

38.—(1) Where in relation to any township the Commission—

(a) either of their own accord or on representations made to them by a crofter who is the tenant of a croft situated in the said township or by the landlord of such a croft or by a grazings committee appointed under section 47 of this Act in respect of common grazings shared in by any such crofter, and

(b) after such consultation as is reasonably practicable with the tenants and the landlords of crofts situated in the township and with any grazings committee appointed as aforesaid, and

(c) after making such inquiries as they think fit,

are satisfied that the township ought to be reorganised in order to secure the preservation or the better development thereof, they may prepare a draft of a scheme (in this Act referred to as a "reorganisation scheme") for the reorganisation of the township.

(2) A reorganisation scheme shall provide for the re-allocation of the land in the township in such manner as is, in the opinion of the Commission, most conducive to the proper and efficient use of that land and to the general benefit of the township, so, however, that under the scheme every crofter who is the tenant of a croft situated in the township and who so wishes shall be granted the tenancy of a croft and that such croft shall—

(a) if the crofter so wishes, include any dwelling-house which formed part of the croft of which he was tenant immediately before the date on which the scheme was put into effect, and

(b) if he so wishes, be of a value not less than that of the croft of which he was tenant as aforesaid.

(3) A reorganisation scheme may, if the Commission think fit, make provision with respect to all or any of the following matters—

(a) the inclusion in the scheme of any land in the vicinity of the township, being land to which this Act does not apply, which in the opinion of the Commission ought to be used for the enlargement of crofts in the township or of common grazings used exclusively or shared in by the township;

(b) the admission into the township of new crofters and the allocation to them of shares in the common grazings;

(c) the apportionment for the exclusive use of the township of a part of any common grazings in which it shares;

(d) the inclusion in any croft formed under the scheme of a part of the common grazings or of any land held runrig;

(e) any other matter incidental to or consequential on the provisions of the scheme.

(4) For the purposes of a reorganisation scheme the Commission shall prepare such maps and plans as may be necessary to indicate the general effect of the scheme and its effects on each of the crofts in the township.

(5) The Commission shall serve on each crofter who is the tenant of a croft situated in the township to which a draft reorganisation scheme relates a copy of such scheme together with a notice—

(a) naming a place within the locality in which the said township is situated where a copy of the maps and plans prepared by the Commission under subsection (4) above may be inspected at all reasonable hours, and

(b) requesting that the crofter on whom the said notice is served shall, within 4 months from the date of such service, intimate to the Commission in writing whether he is in favour of the scheme or not.

Where any crofter on whom such a notice as aforesaid has been served fails to comply with the request contained in such notice, he shall for the purposes of this section be deemed to have intimated to the Commission in compliance with the said request that he is in favour of the scheme.

(6) If within the said period of 4 months a majority of the crofters on whom a copy of a draft reorganisation scheme and notice have been served in pursuance of subsection (5) above have intimated to the Commission in compliance with the request contained in such notice that they are in favour of the scheme, the Commission shall submit to the Secretary of State the draft reorganisation scheme and the maps and plans prepared by them under subsection (4) above together with such information as they may think necessary, or as the Secretary of State may require, for the purpose of informing him of the general purport and effect of the scheme, and shall submit also a statement of their views on the prospects of the development of agricultural and other industries in the township and in the locality in which the township is situated.

(7) The Secretary of State may confirm a draft reorganisation scheme submitted to him under subsection (6) above with or without modifications, and the provisions of Schedule 4 to this Act shall apply with respect to the confirmation and the validity of such a scheme.

Putting into effect of reorganisation schemes

39.—(1) It shall be the duty of the Commission to put into effect any reorganisation scheme confirmed by the Secretary of State under section 38 of this Act, and the Commission may, subject to any directions in that behalf given to them by the Secretary of State, do all such things as may be required for that purpose.

(2) A reorganisation scheme shall be put into effect on such date as may be appointed by the Commission, and the Commission may appoint different dates in respect of different provisions of the scheme, and any reference in this Act to the date on which a reorganisation scheme is put into effect shall, in relation to any land, be construed as a reference to the date on which the provisions of that scheme which apply to such land are put into effect.

(3) The Commission shall, on a reorganisation scheme being confirmed by the Secretary of State, remit the scheme to the Land Court to fix the sums which will become payable on the scheme being put into effect—

(a) to each person who immediately before the said date was the tenant of a croft in the township, by way of compensation in respect of permanent improvements by reason of the termination of his tenancy by virtue of subsection (6) below;

(b) by each person (whether or not he was immediately before the said date the tenant of a croft in the township) who under the scheme becomes the tenant of a croft, in respect of the permanent improvements on that croft; and

(c) by way of rent in respect of each of the crofts formed under the scheme.

(4) In fixing rents under subsection (3)(c) above the Land Court shall so proceed that the aggregate of the rents so fixed, so far as attributable to subjects which formed part of crofts comprised in the township at the date of the confirmation of the scheme—

(a) does not exceed the aggregate of the rents payable in respect of those subjects at that date, and

(b) is fairly apportioned amongst the said subjects.

(5) The rent fixed by the Land Court in pursuance of subsection (3)(c) above in respect of any croft shall not be altered, except by agreement between the landlord and the crofter, for a period of 7 years from the term at which it first became payable.

(6) For the purpose of putting into effect the provisions of a reorganisation scheme, the Commission shall serve on the tenant and on the landlord of every croft to which those provisions apply and on any person (other than such a tenant) who under the scheme is to become the tenant of a croft a notice specifying the date on which the scheme is to be put into effect, and where such notices have been served—

(a) every such tenant shall be deemed to have given notice renouncing the tenancy of his croft immediately before the said date; and

(b) each person (whether or not such a tenant) who under the scheme is to become the tenant of a croft shall on that date become the tenant of that croft.

(7) Where any buildings situated on land to which a reorganisation scheme applies will on the putting into effect of the scheme cease to be required in connection with the occupation of that land, the Commission shall, on the scheme being confirmed by the Secretary of State, give notice to that effect to the landlord of the land, and thereupon subsections (7) and (8) of section 23 of this Act shall apply in relation to the buildings first mentioned as if the said notice had been a notice given under the said subsection (7) to the landlord by the Commission immediately before the date of the putting into effect of the scheme.

A notice given under this subsection to a landlord by the Commission shall inform the landlord of the effect of this subsection in relation to the buildings in respect of which the notice is given.

(8) Where a reorganisation scheme provides, in pursuance of section 38(3) (a) of this Act, for the inclusion in the scheme of land in the vicinity of the township, the Secretary of State shall, on confirming the scheme, serve—

(a) on the occupier of any such land who is not the owner thereof, a copy of the scheme together with a notice terminating his interest in the land on the expiry of 3 months from the date of the service of the notice; and

(b) on the owner of any such land a copy of the scheme together with a notice requiring him to enter into an undertaking that he will, on the date on which the scheme is put into effect, let the land in accordance with the provisions of the scheme.

(9) Where the interest in any land of the occupier of that land is terminated in pursuance of subsection (8)(a) above, the Secretary of State shall be deemed to be authorised to purchase the said interest compulsorily and to have served notice to treat in respect thereof on the date on which the interest is terminated as aforesaid.

(10) Where—

(a) the owner of any land fails within 2 months from the date on which a notice is served on him under paragraph (b) of subsection (8) above to enter into such an undertaking as is mentioned in that paragraph or, having entered into such an undertaking, fails to let the land in accordance with the provisions of the scheme on the date on which the scheme is put into effect; or

(b) the owner of any land to which any provision contained in a reorganisation scheme applies gives to the Secretary of State, within 2 months from the date on which notice of the confirmation of the scheme is served on him under paragraph 7 of Schedule 4 to this Act, notice requiring the Secretary of State to purchase the land;

the Secretary of State shall be deemed to be authorised to purchase the said land compulsorily and to have served notice to treat in respect thereof immediately before the date on which the scheme is put into effect.

Any purchase of land under this subsection shall be deemed to be completed immediately before the date on which the scheme is put into effect, and the Secretary of State shall, as the landlord of such land, be liable to pay or, as the case may be, entitled to receive any such sum as is mentioned in subsection (3)(a) or (b) above which becomes payable on the said date and any sum payable on that date under section 34(1) of this Act by way of compensation for deterioration of, or damage to, fixed equipment on the land.

(11) This section and section 38 of this Act shall, unless the context otherwise requires, apply in relation to a group of neighbouring townships as they apply in relation to a township.

Commission to obtain information and compile register of crofts

Obtaining of information by Commission

40.—(1) The Commission may by notice served on the owner or the occupier of any holding require him to furnish them with such information as may be specified in the notice with regard to the extent, the rent and the tenure of the holding and with regard to such other matters relating to the ownership or the occupation of the holding as the Commission may reasonably require for the execution of their functions under this Act.

(2) If any owner or occupier on whom a notice has been served under subsection (1) above—

    (a) fails without reasonable cause or neglects to furnish to the Commission within 3 months after the service of the notice the information specified in the notice; or

    (b) in furnishing such information as aforesaid knowingly or recklessly furnishes any information which is false in a material particular,

he shall be guilty of an offence and shall be liable on summary conviction to a fine of an amount not exceeding level 1 on the standard scale.

Register of Crofts

41.—(1) It shall be the duty of the Commission to compile and maintain a register of crofts (in this Act referred to as "the Register of Crofts").

(2) There shall be entered in the Register of Crofts—

    (a) the name, location, rent and extent of every croft;

    (b) the name of the tenant and the landlord of each croft;

    (c) any consent of the landlord of a croft under section 50(1)(b) of this Act; and

    (d) such other matters relating to each croft as the Commission may, with the approval of the Secretary of State, decide are proper to be entered in the Register;

and the Commission shall from time to time insert new entries in the Register or alter or omit existing entries so far as may be necessary to ensure the accuracy of the Register and shall send a copy of any new entry, or of any entry altered by them, to the landlord and the tenant of the croft concerned, and shall intimate the omission of any entry to the owner and the tenant (if any) of the land concerned:

Provided that the Commission shall not be required under this subsection to send a copy of any new entry or of any entry altered by them or to intimate the omission of any entry to any person who has to any extent assisted the Commission in the performance of their duties of inserting or, as the case may be, altering or omitting any entry by the furnishing of information to them.

(3) The Commission shall, on a request for an extract of any entry in the Register of Crofts being made to them by a person who, in their opinion, has

good reason for desiring an extract of the said entry, furnish that person with such extract certified by the person for the time being acting as secretary to the Commission; and a document purporting to be an extract of an entry in the Register and to be certified as aforesaid shall be sufficient evidence that the Register contains such an entry.

(4) The register of crofts compiled by the Commission under section 15(2) of the 1955 Act shall, so far as it contains particulars which are required by or under subsection (2) above to be entered in the Register of Crofts, be deemed to have been compiled by the Commission in pursuance of subsection (1) above.

GENERAL NOTE

The fact that a holding has been registered as a croft in the Register of Crofts is purely administrative and does not prove the holding is a croft (see *Elder* v. *Manson* 1964 S.L.T. (Land Ct.) 15).

Financial assistance to crofters, cottars and certain owner-occupiers etc.

Crofters

42.—(1) For the purpose of aiding and developing agricultural production on crofts, the Secretary of State may, after consultation with the Commission and with the approval of the Treasury, make schemes for providing grants and loans to crofters.

(2) Any scheme under subsection (1) above may—

(a) provide for the administration, through the agency of the Commission, of the grants and loans payable thereunder;

(b) make provision enabling the Secretary of State to recover the grant or loan in such circumstances and from such person as may be specified in the scheme;

(c) provide that, where the grant or loan is being given in respect of a common grazing and a grazings committee or a grazings constable has been appointed under section 47 of this Act, the Secretary of State shall pay the grant or loan to the clerk of the grazings committee or the constable for the benefit of the crofters concerned.

(3) Any scheme under subsection (1) above shall be embodied in a statutory instrument which shall be laid before Parliament after being made, and any such scheme may be varied or revoked by a subsequent scheme made in the like manner.

(4) The Secretary of State may, in accordance with arrangements made by him with the approval of the Treasury, provide assistance by way of grants or loans or by the supply for payment in cash of building or other materials towards the erection or improvement or rebuilding of dwelling-houses and other buildings for crofters or towards the provision or improvement of roads, or water or electricity or gas supplies.

(5) The Secretary of State may, in accordance with arrangements made by him with the approval of the Treasury, provide assistance by way of loan to the incoming tenant of a croft to enable him to pay to the outgoing tenant of the croft or the landlord thereof the compensation for permanent improvements due to such outgoing tenant.

(6) Regulations shall be made by the Secretary of State—

(a) for securing that, where a grant has been made towards the erection, improvement or rebuilding of a dwelling-house or other building, conditions with respect to the occupation and maintenance thereof shall apply thereto for such period from the completion of the work (not being longer than 40 years) as may be specified in the regulations;

(b) for securing that in the event of a breach of any of the conditions the Secretary of State may recover from such person as may be specified in the regulations a sum bearing the same proportion to the grant made as the period between the date of the breach of the condition and the expiration of the period specified under paragraph (a) above bears to the last mentioned period, together with interest on such sum from the date on which the grant was made at such a rate as may be specified in the regulations;

(c) for providing that the conditions applied by the regulations to a dwelling-house or building shall cease to apply on payment to the Secretary of State by such person as may be specified in the regulations of such amount as may be so specified;

(d) for securing that, where any conditions apply to a dwelling-house or building by virtue of the regulations, the Secretary of State shall cause to be recorded in the Register of Sasines or, as the case may be, registered in the Land Register of Scotland a notice in a form prescribed by the regulations specifying the conditions which by virtue of the regulations apply to the dwelling-house or building; and that, where such conditions cease so to apply by virtue of such a payment to the Secretary of State as is referred to in paragraph (c) above, the Secretary of State shall cause to be so recorded or registered a notice in a form prescribed as aforesaid stating that the conditions no longer apply to the dwelling-house or building;

(e) for such other incidental and supplementary matters as appear to the Secretary of State to be requisite or expedient for the purposes aforesaid.

(7) The Secretary of State may make regulations providing that the conditions applied to any dwelling-house by regulations made under subsection (6) above shall not apply to such dwelling-house in such circumstances and to such extent as may be specified in the regulations made under this subsection.

(8) No assistance by way of grant shall be given under subsection (4) above towards the erection, improvement or rebuilding of any dwelling-house or other building or towards the provision or improvement of roads, or water or electricity or gas supplies if assistance out of public money by way of grant or subsidy has been given under any other enactment towards the works in question.

(9) A person shall not be disqualified for receiving assistance under subsection (4) above by reason only that, after he has applied for and the Secretary of State has undertaken to provide such assistance, he has become the owner of the croft in respect of which the application was made.

(10) If any person, for the purpose of obtaining for himself or any other person a grant or loan under a scheme made under subsection (1) above or under subsection (4) above, knowingly or recklessly makes a false statement he shall be guilty of an offence and shall be liable on summary conviction to a fine of an amount not exceeding level 5 on the standard scale.

GENERAL NOTE
Subsection (2)(b) and (c) gives effect to recommendations of the Scottish Law Commission.

Supplementary provisions as to loans under s.42

43.—(1) Where assistance is given under section 42(4) or (5) of this Act by way of loan, the following provisions of this section shall have effect.

(2) The Secretary of State shall give notice to the landlord of the giving of any such assistance as aforesaid.

(3) The agreement for the loan shall be sent to the principal clerk of the Land Court to be recorded in the Crofters Holdings Book and as recorded shall have the effect of transferring to the Secretary of State all rights of the crofter and his statutory successors to compensation for permanent improvements up to the amount of any outstanding liability to the Secretary of State.

(4) Any amount due by virtue of subsection (3) above to the Secretary of State by the landlord may, if the Secretary of State on the application of the landlord so determines, be deemed to be a loan by the Secretary of State to the landlord, and Schedule 5 to this Act shall apply in relation thereto.

(5) Where the outgoing tenant of a croft is under any liability to the Secretary of State in respect of a loan made to him, the Secretary of State and the incoming tenant may agree that the latter shall assume such liability, and if they so agree the amount thereof shall be deemed to be a loan made to the incoming tenant under section 42(5) of this Act and this section shall have effect accordingly.

(6) Schedule 5 to this Act shall apply in relation to any loan made by virtue of section 42(9) of this Act.

Cottars

44. The Secretary of State shall have the like powers to provide assistance by way of loan, grant and the supply of building or other materials for the erection, improvement or rebuilding of dwelling-houses and other buildings for cottars as he has to provide assistance for the erection, improvement or rebuilding of dwelling-houses and other buildings for crofters, and subsections (4), (6), (8), (9) and (10) of section 42 of this Act shall apply accordingly.

Former crofters and cottars who have acquired site of the dwelling-house

45.—(1) The Secretary of State may provide assistance under section 42(4) of this Act but not in respect of buildings other than dwelling-houses to—
  (a) a person, being a crofter who has acquired the site of the dwelling-house on or pertaining to his croft after 10th June 1976;
  (b) the nominee of such a person, being a member of his family, to whom the site was conveyed by the landlord of the croft;
  (c) a member of such a person's family who has acquired the title to the site from that person or such nominee;
  (d) a person, being a cottar who has acquired the site of the dwelling-house on or pertaining to his subject after 10th June 1976,
for a period of 7 years from the date of the acquisition from the landlord.

(2) Schedule 5 to this Act shall apply in relation to any loan made under section 42(4) of this Act by virtue of subsection (1) above.

(3) Where a person other than the landlord was infeft in the site of the dwelling-house immediately before the conveyance, the reference in subsection (1)(b) above to the landlord shall be construed as a reference to the landlord and such other person for their respective rights.

(4) If any person, referred to in any of paragraphs (a) to (d) of subsection (1) above, for the purpose of obtaining for himself or any other person a grant or loan under section 42(4) of this Act, knowingly or recklessly makes a false statement he shall be guilty of an offence and shall be liable on summary conviction to a fine of an amount not exceeding level 5 on the standard scale.

Owner-occupiers of like economic status as crofters and other persons

46.—(1) The Secretary of State shall have the like powers to provide assistance by way of loan, grant and the supply of building or other materials for the erection, improvement or rebuilding of buildings other than dwelling-houses or towards the provision or improvement of roads, or water or electricity or gas supplies for owners of holdings to which subsection (2) below applies as he has to provide such assistance for crofters; and subsections (4), (6), (8) and (10) of section 42 of this Act shall apply accordingly.

(2) This subsection applies to any holding which—
  (a) is situated in the crofting counties; and
  (b) is either—
      (i) a holding of which the area does not exceed 30 hectares, or

(ii) a holding of which the annual rent, if it were a croft let to a crofter under this Act, would not in the opinion of the Secretary of State exceed £100, or

(iii) a holding which exceeds 30 hectares and of which the annual rent if it were a croft so let would in the opinion of the Secretary of State exceed £100, but which in the opinion of the Secretary of State is not substantially larger than 30 hectares or is capable of being let as a croft at an annual rent not substantially in excess of £100; and

(c) is owned by a person who in the opinion of the Secretary of State is of substantially the same economic status as a crofter; and

(d) is occupied by the owner thereof.

(3) Schedule 5 to this Act shall apply in relation to any loan made to the owner of a holding under subsection (1) above.

(4) The Secretary of State shall have the like power to provide financial assistance—

(a) for occupiers of crofts who are also the owners thereof and who in the opinion of the Secretary of State are of substantially the same economic status as a crofter; and

(b) for occupiers of holdings, other than crofts, situated in the crofting counties which are either holdings of which the area does not exceed 30 hectares (exclusive of any common pasture or grazing held therewith) or holdings the annual rent of which, if they were crofts let to crofters under this Act, would not, in the opinion of the Secretary of State, exceed £100, being occupiers who in the opinion of the Secretary of State are of substantially the same economic status as a crofter; and

(c) for occupiers of holdings, other than crofts, situated in the crofting counties which exceed 30 hectares (exclusive of any common pasture or grazing held therewith) and of which the annual rent if they were crofts so let would in the opinion of the Secretary of State exceed £100, but which in the opinion of the Secretary of State are not substantially larger than 30 hectares (exclusive of any common pasture or grazing held therewith) or are capable of being so let at an annual rent not substantially in excess of £100, being occupiers who in the opinion of the Secretary of State are of substantially the same economic status as a crofter; and

(d) for subtenants of crofts or parts of crofts occupying under subleases intimated or granted as mentioned in section 29(2) of this Act,

as he has by virtue of subsection (1) of section 42 of this Act to provide financial assistance for crofters; and accordingly the said subsection (1) shall have effect as if the reference therein to crofts included a reference to such holdings and to parts of crofts and as if the reference therein to crofters included a reference to occupiers of crofts who are also the owners thereof, to occupiers of such holdings and to subtenants of crofts or parts of crofts.

(5) If any person, for the purpose of obtaining for himself or any other person, a grant or loan under a scheme made under section 42(1) of this Act as applied by subsection (4) above, knowingly or recklessly makes a false statement he shall be guilty of an offence and shall be liable on summary conviction to a fine of an amount not exceeding level 5 on the standard scale.

Common Grazings

Appointment, etc., of grazings committee or grazings constable

47.—(1) The crofters who share in a common grazing may from time to time, at a public meeting called in accordance with subsection (2) below, appoint a grazings committee of such number as the meeting shall decide; and a person may be appointed to be a member of a grazings committee notwithstanding that he is not a crofter.

(2) Notice of a meeting for the appointment of a grazings committee may be given by any two crofters interested in the common grazing and shall be given by notice published in each of two successive weeks in one or more newspapers circulating in the district in which the township is situated or by notice posted for two successive weeks in such public place or places in that district as may be approved by the Commission.

(3) If the crofters who share in a common grazing fail at any time to appoint a grazings committee, the Commission may, after making such inquiry, if any, as they may deem necessary, appoint a grazings committee, or may appoint a person to be grazings constable; and a committee or constable so appointed shall have the like powers and duties as a grazings committee appointed under subsection (1) above.

(4) The term of office of the members of a grazings committee appointed under this section shall be 3 years, and at the expiry of that period a new grazings committee shall be appointed as aforesaid. A retiring member of a committee shall be eligible for re-election.

(5) A majority of the members of a grazings committee shall be a quorum; and any vacancy occurring in the membership of a grazings committee by reason of the death or resignation of a member shall be filled by nomination of the remaining members.

(6) A grazings committee appointed under subsection (1) above, or in the case of a grazings committee appointed under subsection (3) above the Commission, shall appoint some person, whether a member of the committee or not, to be the clerk of the committee.

(7) The term of office of a grazings constable appointed by the Commission under subsection (3) above shall be such as may be specified in the instrument by which he is appointed, and he shall receive such annual remuneration as the Commission may determine; and such remuneration shall be defrayed by an assessment levied in such manner as the Commission may deem reasonable on the crofters who share in the common grazing.

(8) If the Commission are satisfied, after making such inquiry, if any, as they may deem necessary, that any or all of the members or the clerk of a grazings committee (however appointed under this section) are not properly carrying out the duties imposed on them under this Act, the Commission may remove from office any or all such members or such clerk and may appoint or provide for the appointment of other persons (whether crofters or not) in their or his place.

(9) A grazings committee shall pay such annual remuneration to the clerk appointed under subsection (6) or (8) above as they may determine; and they may recover from the crofters sharing in the common grazings all expenditure incurred by them in paying such remuneration.

(10) For the purposes of the application of this Act to common grazings, any reference therein to a crofter shall include a reference to any person who, not being a crofter, is entitled to share in a common grazing along with crofters.

GENERAL NOTE

No definition of "common grazing" is given. However the recent judgment of the full court in *Macdonald* v. *Prentice's Trustees* 1993 S.L.T. (Land Ct.) 60 at p.65 contains valuable guidance on the difference between a crofter's right in a common grazing and a crofter's right of grazing forming a pertinent of his croft.

Powers and duties of grazings committees

48.—(1) It shall be the duty of a grazings committee—
(a) to maintain the common grazings and to provide, maintain and, if necessary, replace the fixed equipment required in connection therewith;

(b) to carry out works for the improvement of such grazings and equipment;

(c) to make and administer, with a view to their due observance, regulations (in this Act referred to as "common grazings regulations") with respect to the management and use of the common grazings:

Provided that nothing in paragraph (a) or (b) above shall preclude a grazings committee from performing the duties therein specified on land other than the common grazings.

(2) The grazings committee shall give notice to each crofter sharing in the common grazings of any proposals to carry out works in pursuance of the duty imposed by subsection (1)(b) above, or to plant trees under subsection (4) below, and the proposed allocation of the expenditure to be incurred in respect of those works or, as the case may be, that planting among such crofters; and any such crofter may within one month of the date of such notice make representations in respect of the proposals or the proposed allocation to the Commission who may approve the proposals or proposed allocation with or without modifications or reject them.

(3) Notwithstanding section 29(2) of this Act, subsection (2) above shall have effect in a case where such a right is sublet as if any reference to a crofter included a reference to a crofter in whose place a subtenant has come; but no liability to meet expenditure incurred by a grazings committee in the performance of the duties imposed on them by subsection (1)(b) above shall be imposed on such a crofter in respect of any period during which such a subtenancy subsists.

(4) Subject to section 50 of this Act and to subsections (5) and (6) below, where the grazings committee have obtained the approval and consent referred to in subsection (1) of that section they may plant trees on, and use as woodlands, any part of the common grazing in accordance with the approval and consent.

(5) Where any crofter interested in the common grazing requests them to do so, the grazings committee shall exercise their power under subsection (4) above.

(6) The power of the grazings committee under subsection (4) above shall not be exercised in such a way that the whole of the common grazing is planted with trees and used as woodlands.

(7) A person appointed by the Commission shall have power to summon and to attend any meeting of a grazings committee for the purpose of advising them and otherwise assisting them in the performance of their duties.

Common grazings regulations

49.—(1) Every grazings committee shall, within 6 months after being required by the Commission so to do, make and submit to the Commission common grazings regulations.

(2) Without prejudice to the generality of the power conferred on a grazings committee by section 48(1)(c) of this Act, common grazings regulations shall make provision with respect to the following matters—

(a) the recovery by the grazings committee from the crofters sharing in the common grazings of all expenses incurred by the committee in maintaining the common grazings and in providing, maintaining or replacing any fixed equipment required in connection therewith;

(b) the recovery by the grazings committee from such crofters of all expenses incurred by the committee in the performance of the duties imposed on them by subsection (1)(b), and the exercise of their powers under subsection (4), of section 48 of this Act according to the proposed allocation of expenditure referred to in subsection (2) of that section or, as the case may be, that allocation as approved or modified by the Commission under that subsection;

(c) the levying by the grazings committee on, and the recovery by them from, the crofters referred to in paragraph (a) above or, as the case may be, such of the crofters referred to in paragraph (b) above as are liable to pay any expenses as mentioned in that paragraph, in such proportions as may be specified in the regulations, such sums as will in the opinion of the committee be necessary to enable the committee to meet any expenses which they may incur in the performance of the duties imposed on them by paragraphs (a) and (b) respectively of section 48(1) of this Act;

(d) the number and the kind of stock which each crofter is entitled to put on the common grazings;

(e) the alteration of individual soumings where works for the improvement of the common grazings or the fixed equipment required in connection therewith have been carried out and all the crofters have not contributed to the expenses incurred in carrying out such works;

(f) where appropriate, the cutting of peats and the collection of seaweed;

(g) subject to the provisions of this Act, the summoning of meetings of the grazings committee and the procedure and conduct of business at such meetings.

(3) Common grazings regulations may—

(a) restrict the use of any part of the common grazings on which works of improvement have been carried out to crofters who contribute towards the expenses incurred by the common grazings committee in carrying out those works;

(b) where the use of any part of the common grazings is restricted as aforesaid, regulate the number and kinds of stock which each contributing crofter may put on that part and the number and kinds of stock which each crofter (whether or not he is a contributing crofter) may put on the remainder of the common grazings.

(4) Common grazings regulations made by a grazings committee shall be of no effect unless confirmed by the Commission. The Commission may confirm with or without modification or refuse to confirm any common grazings regulations submitted to them for confirmation, and may fix the date on which the regulations are to come into operation; and if no date is so fixed, the regulations shall come into operation at the expiration of one month from the date of their confirmation.

(5) If a grazings committee fail within the time limited by subsection (1) above to make and submit to the Commission common grazings regulations or to make and submit to the Commission common grazings regulations which in the opinion of the Commission are sufficient and satisfactory, the Commission may themselves make such common grazings regulations, which shall have the like force and effect as if they had been made by the grazings committee and confirmed by the Commission.

(6) A grazings committee may from time to time, and, if so required by the Commission, shall within the time limited by such requirement, make further regulations amending the common grazings regulations for the time being in force, and subsections (4) and (5) above shall apply to any such amending regulations subject to any necessary modifications.

(7) Before confirming, making or amending regulations in accordance with the foregoing provisions of this section, the Commission shall consult the landlord of the common grazings to which the regulations relate; and the Commission shall send a copy of any regulations so confirmed, made or amended to the landlord and to the grazings committee.

(8) Common grazings regulations for the time being in force under this section shall have effect notwithstanding anything contrary thereto or incon-

sistent therewith contained in any lease or other agreement, whether entered into before or after the coming into force of such regulations.

Use of common grazings for forestry purposes

50.—(1) Where a grazings committee or any crofter interested in the common grazing proposes that the committee should, in exercise of their power under section 48(4) of this Act, plant trees on, and use as woodlands, any part of the common grazing, the committee shall apply for—

   (a) the approval of the Commission; and

   (b) the consent of the landlord of the common grazing,

to the use as woodlands of the part of the common grazing concerned.

   (2) A landlord's consent—

   (a) shall be in writing;

   (b) shall specify the part of the common grazing to which it relates;

   (c) shall be intimated to the Commission by the landlord or the grazings committee;

   (d) shall not take effect until it is entered in the Register of Crofts; and

   (e) shall, when entered in that Register, be binding on the successors to the landlord's interest.

   (3) A landlord's consent shall cease to have effect if the grazings committee have not commenced planting of trees on the part of the common grazing to which the consent relates on the expiry of the period of seven years beginning with the date on which the consent is entered in the Register of Crofts.

   (4) In this section—

     "landlord's consent" means the consent of the landlord referred to in subsection (1)(b) above; and

     "Register of Crofts" means the Register maintained under section 41 of this Act.

GENERAL NOTE

The Crofter Forestry (Scotland) Act 1991 was introduced to enable crofters to use their land "for forestry purposes". Despite this, it is doubtful whether, unless they receive the specific permission of their landlord to do so, crofters who plant trees are entitled either to cut them down or to sell the timber produced. This anomaly was acknowledged by the Crofters Commission in their "Guide to Crofter Forestry" (Inverness, 1992, para. 1.4) which states that the 1991 Act only provided for Grazings Committees to *use the land as woodlands*. The lack of a definition for the term "woodlands" is likely to cause difficulties in the future. The Commission therefore advises crofters who are seeking the consent of their landlord to plant trees also to seek his agreement, in writing, to cut, take and eventually sell these trees as timber. It is settled law in Scotland that an agricultural tenant cannot cut down any trees on his farm, for these trees are the property of the landlord. The term "woodland" was defined in 1914 when the Land Court thought that the expression was used there in its ordinary meaning, namely, "land which is appropriated or principally used for growing timber, though it may be incidentally or occasionally used for pasture, and which is reserved, replanted at regular intervals, and protected for that purpose" (*Board of Agriculture for Scotland* v. *Macdonald* 1914 S.L.C.R. 43 at p.45). Whilst this referred to land used as woodland by a landowner, it seems probable that this definition would extend to and define the phraseology of s.50.

Unlike most other types of tenant, a crofter is entitled (and expected) to improve his subjects for his own benefit. This may include not just agricultural works but also the provision of his own dwelling-house and buildings for auxiliary occupations (see s.31). The permanent improvements to be considered for compensation when a crofter leaves his croft will include the planting of trees (Sched. 3, para. 8). However, trees planted on common grazings under s.48(4) are to be excluded from such compensation.

It would come as a surprise to most crofters who had planted trees on their own land if they were to be prevented from felling them and, still worse, from disposing of them as their own. As in many other crofting matters, the law of Scotland applicable to the crofters' situation has evolved along lines which strengthen the position of the landowner against that of an agricultural tenant. Thus, where a tenant of a farm is not entitled to cut down trees, a crofter is likewise forbidden by law to do so without his landlord's written permission. It is arguable that, in this matter, the law of agricultural tenancies is out of step with what Parliament intended to apply to crofting. The general law does not make any concession for the permanent nature of a crofter's tenancy, his security of tenure, and the fact that few landowners have little more than a remote involvement in the activities of their crofting tenants. As with other improvements on his croft for which he might be compensated, the onus lies on the crofter to show proof that any trees claimed by him were planted by himself or his predecessors in the tenancy. However, as to the general law of property in timber, there is no doubt that in a lease of lands the lessor's rights are limited to those yearly fruits which either naturally or by the lessor's industry spring up from the surface. He is not entitled to any of the woods or growing timber above ground. Indeed the statutory conditions of tenure of a crofter provide that:

"The crofter shall permit the landlord or any person authorised by the landlord in that behalf to enter upon the croft for the purpose of exercising ... any of the following rights ... cutting or taking timber ... excepting timber and other trees planted by the crofter or any of his predecessors in the tenancy, or which may be necessary for ornament or shelter" (Sched. 2, para. 11(d)).

Crofters wishing to take part in commercial forestry must therefore obtain much more than the consent of their landlord to plant trees on, and use as woodlands, any part of the common grazing despite having the Commission's approval and the landlord's consent. In recognition of these difficulties, the Crofters Commission along with the Scottish Crofters Union, the National Farmers Union of Scotland and the Scottish Landowners' Federation have been obliged to prepare a model form of agreement and consent incorporating a Schedule of Standard Conditions including the right of the crofters to cut, take and sell their own trees. Copies of the form are available from the Crofters Commission, 4/6 Castle Wynd, Inverness.

Enlargement of common grazings

51.—(1) Where the owner of any land to which this Act does not apply agrees to grant rights in any pasture or grazing land to the crofters sharing in any common grazing and that owner and the crofters agree that such land will form part of the said common grazing, then as from the date on which such rights are first exercisable by the crofters, the land shall form part of the common grazing, and this Act shall apply accordingly to the common grazing as so enlarged.

(2) The owner of any land which becomes part of a common grazing by virtue of subsection (1) above shall give notice to the Commission of the enlargement of that common grazing.

Miscellaneous provisions as to common grazings, as to lands held runrig, and as to use by crofters of peat bogs, etc.

52.—(1) Any person who contravenes or fails to comply with any common grazings regulations for the time being in force under section 49 of this Act shall be guilty of an offence and shall be liable on summary conviction to a fine of an amount not exceeding level 1 on the standard scale; and in the case of a continuing offence to a further fine not exceeding 50 pence for each day on which the offence is continued after the grazings committee or the Commission have served notice on him warning him of the offence.

(2) Where it is prescribed by the common grazings regulations applicable to the common grazings of a township that the right of a crofter to share in such grazings shall be conditional on his making his croft available during the winter season for the accommodation of any stock belonging to other persons sharing in such grazings, any crofter may apply to the grazings committee for their consent to the exclusion of such stock from his croft or from part thereof, and if he is dissatisfied with the decision of the committee on such application he may appeal therefrom to the Commission.

Any consent given under this subsection by a grazings committee or, on appeal, by the Commission may be given subject to such conditions, if any, as the committee or the Commission, as the case may be, may think proper.

(3) The Commission may, on the application of any crofters interested, after consultation with the grazings committee, apportion a common grazing

shared by two or more townships into separate parts for the exclusive use of the several townships or may apportion a part of such grazing for the exclusive use of one of the townships.

(4) The Commission may, on the application of any crofter interested, after consultation with the grazings committee, apportion a part of a common grazing (including the site of the dwelling-house of the crofter so applying if situated on the common grazing), other than a part on which the grazings committee have planted trees and which they are using as woodlands under section 48(4) of this Act, for the exclusive use of the applicant.

(5) An application under subsection (4) above shall be competent notwithstanding that every part of the grazing except the part in respect of which the application is made has already been apportioned under that subsection.

(6) Where the Commission in pursuance of subsection (3) or (4) above apportion to a township or to an individual a part of a common grazing for its or his exclusive use, they may make the apportionment subject to such conditions, including conditions with respect to the fencing or the draining of the apportioned part, as they may think fit.

(7) Notwithstanding anything in the Ground Game Act 1880, it shall be lawful for the crofters interested in a common grazing or in a part of a common grazing apportioned under subsection (3) above—

(a) to appoint not more than two of their number; and
(b) to authorise in writing one person bona fide employed by them for reward,

to kill and take ground game on the common grazing or the part thereof, as the case may be; and for the purposes of the said Act of 1880 any person appointed as aforesaid shall be deemed to be the occupier of the common grazing or the part thereof, but shall not have the right to authorise any other person to kill and take ground game, and any person authorised as aforesaid shall be deemed to have been authorised by the occupier of the common grazing or the part thereof to kill and take ground game with firearms or otherwise.

(8) The Commission may, on the application of any landlord or crofter interested, apportion lands held runrig among the holders thereof in such manner and subject to such conditions as appears to the Commission in the circumstances of the case to be just and expedient.

(9) The Commission may draw up a scheme regulating the use by crofters on the same estate of peat bogs, or of seaweed for the reasonable purposes of their crofts, or of heather or grass used for thatching purposes, and the charge for the use of all or any of these may be included in the rents fixed for the crofts.

GENERAL NOTE

Where a croft house is situated on a common grazing, it is appropriate that an apportionment be sought so that the site of the dwelling-house is to be for the exclusive use of the applicant. That this is competent is clarified in subs. (4) as recommended by the Scottish Law Commission.

Where all the shares in a common grazing, except that of the applicant, have already been apportioned, the grazing can no longer be regarded as common. It is provided in s.3(4)(b) that part of a common grazing which has been apportioned for the exclusive use of a crofter under s.52(4) becomes part of the croft, which effectively turns a right to graze into the right to work the apportioned land fully by ploughing, cropping and for other uses. Subsection (5) clarifies that one remaining shareholder should have the right to apply for apportionment of his share[s] as recommended by the Scottish Law Commission.

Provisions relating to Land Court

Jurisdictional provisions

53.—(1) Without prejudice to any jurisdiction exercisable by it under any enactment, the Land Court shall have power to determine, either on the application of any person having an interest or on a reference made to it by

the Commission, any question of fact or law arising under this Act including, without prejudice to the said generality—
  (a) the question whether any holding is a croft;
  (b) the question who is the tenant of any croft;
  (c) any question as to the boundaries of a croft or of any pasture or grazing land a right in which forms part of a croft;
  (d) the question whether any land is or forms part of a common pasture or grazing to which this Act applies:
Provided that the Land Court shall not have power under this subsection to determine—
  (i) any question of a kind reserved by this Act to a court other than the Land Court; or
  (ii) any question (other than a question of law) decided by the Secretary of State or the Commission in the discharge of any of his or their functions under this Act.
(2) The Land Court shall cause intimation to be made to the Commission of its determination on any question coming before it under this Act.

GENERAL NOTE

An order or determination of the Land Court may be enforced as if it were a decree of the sheriff having jurisdiction in the area where the order or determination is to be enforced (Scottish Land Court Act 1993, Sched. 1, para. 16). An interested party may obtain an extract of any order (provided the period of appeal has elapsed) which will include a warrant for execution. Applications should be made to the Principal Clerk, Scottish Land Court, 1 Grosvenor Crescent, Edinburgh.

Crofters Holdings Book

54. The principal clerk of the Land Court shall keep a book called the "Crofters Holdings Book" in which he shall record—
  (a) anything sent to him by the Commission in accordance with section 2(3) of this Act,
  (b) any agreement for a loan sent to him under section 43(3) of this Act.

Miscellaneous and General Provisions

Service of notices

55.—(1) Any notice for the purposes of this Act shall be in writing, and any notice or other document required or authorised by or under this Act to be given to or served on any person shall be duly given or served if it is delivered to him or left at his proper address or sent to him by post.

(2) Where any notice or other document is to be given to or served on a person as being the person having any interest in land and it is not practicable after reasonable inquiry to ascertain his name or address, the notice or document may be given or served by addressing it to him by the description of the person having that interest in the land (naming it) and delivering the notice or document to some responsible person on the land or by affixing it, or a copy of it, to some conspicuous object on the land.

Provisions as to entry and inspection

56.—(1) Any person authorised by the Secretary of State or the Commission in that behalf shall have power at all reasonable times to enter on and inspect any land for the purpose of determining whether, and if so in what manner, any of the powers conferred on the Secretary of State or the Commission by this Act are to be exercised in relation to the land, or whether, and if so in what manner, any direction given under any such power has been complied with.

(2) Any person authorised as aforesaid who proposes to exercise any power of entry or inspection conferred by this Act shall if so required prod-

uce some duly authenticated document showing his authority to exercise the power.

(3) Admission to any land shall not be demanded as of right in the exercise of any such power as aforesaid unless in the case of land being used for residential purposes 7 days, or in the case of any other land 24 hours, notice of the intended entry has been given to the occupier of the land.

(4) Any person who obstructs any person authorised by the Secretary of State or the Commission exercising any such power as aforesaid shall be guilty of an offence and shall be liable on summary conviction to a fine of an amount not exceeding level 1 on the standard scale.

Provisions as to compulsory purchase of land and as to management of land

57.—(1) Where by virtue of any provision of this Act the Secretary of State is deemed to be authorised to purchase land compulsorily, then in relation to any such compulsory purchase the Lands Clauses Acts and other enactments mentioned in Part I of Schedule 2 to the Acquisition of Land (Authorisation Procedure) (Scotland) Act 1947, shall be incorporated in accordance with the provisions of the said Part I as if the Secretary of State had been authorised under section 1 of that Act to purchase the land compulsorily; and the Land Compensation (Scotland) Act 1963 shall have effect in relation to any such compulsory purchase subject to the provisions of Part II of that Schedule, of the proviso to section 23(9) of this Act and of subsection (2) below.

(2) The power conferred by section 39 of the Land Compensation (Scotland) Act 1963 to withdraw a notice to treat shall not be exercisable in the case of a notice to treat which is deemed to have been served by virtue of section 23(9) or 39(9) or (10) of this Act.

(3) The Secretary of State may manage, farm, sell, let or otherwise deal with or dispose of land acquired by him under this Act in such manner as appears to him expedient for the purpose for which it was acquired.

Provisions as to representations

58.—(1) Any enactment in this Act providing, in relation to the taking of any action by the Secretary of State, for his taking the action after affording to a person an opportunity of making representations to the Secretary of State shall be construed as a provision that the Secretary of State shall comply with the following requirements.

(2) The Secretary of State shall give notice to the said person specifying the matter under consideration and informing him of the effect of subsection (3) below.

(3) A person to whom notice is given as aforesaid may within the time specified in the notice make representations to the Secretary of State in writing, and, whether or not representations are made to the Secretary of State in writing, may within the time so specified require that an opportunity be afforded to him of being heard by a person appointed by the Secretary of State for the purpose; and, if he so requires, such an opportunity shall be afforded to him and, on the same occasion, to any other person to whom under the enactment referred to in subsection (1) above the Secretary of State is required to afford such an opportunity, and the Secretary of State shall not take action in relation to the matter until he has considered any representations made as aforesaid.

(4) Where any enactment in this Act provides in relation to the taking of any action by the Commission for their taking the action after affording to a person an opportunity of making representations to them, the provisions of this section shall have effect in relation thereto with the substitution for references to the Secretary of State of references to the Commission.

Financial provisions

59.—(1) The expenses of the Commission shall be defrayed by the Secretary of State.

(2) All expenses incurred by the Secretary of State under the provisions of this Act shall be defrayed out of moneys provided by Parliament.

(3) All sums received by the Secretary of State under the provisions of this Act shall be paid into the Consolidated Fund.

Regulations

60. Any regulations made by the Secretary of State under this Act shall be embodied in a statutory instrument which shall be subject to annulment in pursuance of a resolution of either House of Parliament.

Interpretation

61.—(1) In this Act, unless the context otherwise requires—

"the 1955 Act" means the Crofters (Scotland) Act 1955;

"the 1964 Act" means the Succession (Scotland) Act 1964;

"the 1972 Act" means the Town and Country Planning (Scotland) Act 1972;

"authority possessing compulsory purchase powers" has the same meaning as in the 1972 Act;

"the Commission" means the Crofters Commission;

"cottar" has the meaning assigned by section 12(5) of this Act;

"croft" and "crofter" have the meanings assigned to them respectively by section 3 of this Act;

"crofting counties" means the former counties of Argyll, Caithness, Inverness, Orkney, Ross and Cromarty, Sutherland and Zetland;

"croft land" has the meaning assigned to it by section 12(3) of this Act;

"development" has the same meaning as in section 19 of the 1972 Act, except that it includes the operations and uses of land referred to in paragraphs (a) and (e) of subsection (2) of that section;

"fixed equipment" has the like meaning as in the Agricultural Holdings (Scotland) Act 1991;

"functions" includes powers and duties;

"Land Court" means the Scottish Land Court;

"landlord" means—

(a) in relation to a croft, any person for the time being entitled to receive the rents and profits, or to take possession of, the croft;

(b) in relation to the site of the dwelling-house on or pertaining to the subject of a cottar—

(i) where the cottar is the tenant of the subject, any person for the time being entitled to receive the rents and profits, or to take possession of the site, and

(ii) where the cottar is the occupier of the subject who pays no rent, the owner thereof;

"National Trust for Scotland" means the National Trust for Scotland for Places of Historic Interest or Natural Beauty incorporated by the Order confirmed by the National Trust for Scotland Order Confirmation Act 1935;

"permanent improvement" shall be construed in accordance with section 30(7) of this Act;

"prescribed" means prescribed by regulations made by the Secretary of State;

"predecessors in the tenancy" means in relation to a crofter the persons who before him have been tenants of the croft since it was last vacant;

"statutory successor" means any person who under this Act has succeeded or may succeed to a croft whether as a person to whom the tenancy of the croft has been transferred in pursuance of section 16(2) of the 1964 Act or as the executor, heir-at-law, legatee or assignee of his immediate predecessor being a crofter in occupation of the croft;

"the site of the dwelling-house" has the meaning assigned to it by section 12(4) of this Act;

"Whitsunday" and "Martinmas" mean respectively 28th May and 28th November.

(2) Any reference in this Act to a member of a person's or crofter's or former crofter's or deceased crofter's family is a reference to the wife or husband of that person or crofter or former crofter or deceased crofter or his son-in-law or daughter-in-law or anyone who would be, or would in any circumstances have been, entitled to succeed to his estate on intestacy by virtue of the 1964 Act.

Application of Act to Crown

62. This Act shall apply to land an interest in which belongs to Her Majesty in right of the Crown and land an interest in which belongs to a government department or is held in trust for Her Majesty for the purposes of a government department, but in its application to any land an interest in which belongs or is held as aforesaid this Act shall have effect subject to such modifications as may be prescribed.

Transitional provisions and savings, and repeals

63.—(1) The transitional provisions and savings contained in Schedule 6 to this Act shall have effect.

(2) The enactments—

(a) specified in Part I of Schedule 7 to this Act so far as they apply in the crofting counties;

(b) specified in Part II of that Schedule,

are hereby repealed to the extent specified in column 3 of that Schedule.

Short title, commencement and extent

64.—(1) This Act may be cited as the Crofters (Scotland) Act 1993.

(2) Subject to section 28(17) of this Act, this Act shall come into operation on the expiration of 2 months commencing with the date on which it is passed.

(3) This Act extends to Scotland only.

GENERAL NOTE
The Act (other than s.28) came into force on January 5, 1994.

SCHEDULES

SCHEDULE 1

PROVISIONS AS TO THE CROFTERS COMMISSION

Constitution of the Commission

1. The Commission shall be a body corporate and shall have a common seal.

2. Every member of the Commission shall hold and vacate office in accordance with the terms of the instrument under which he is appointed; but notwithstanding anything in such an instru-

ment any member of the Commission may resign his office by a notice given under his hand to the Secretary of State, and a member of the Commission who ceases to hold office shall be eligible for re-appointment to the Commission.

3. The Secretary of State shall pay to the members of the Commission such remuneration and such allowances as he may, with the approval of the Treasury, determine.

4. The Secretary of State shall, in the case of any member of the Commission to whom he may with the approval of the Treasury determine that this paragraph applies, pay such pension, allowance or gratuity to or in respect of the member on his retirement or death, or make such payments towards the provision of such a pension, allowance or gratuity, as he may, with the like approval, determine.

5. If a person ceases to be a member of the Commission and it appears to the Secretary of State that there are special circumstances which make it right that that person should receive compensation he may, with the approval of the Treasury, pay to that person a sum of such amount as he may, with the like approval, determine.

Meetings and Proceedings of the Commission

6. The quorum of the Commission shall be three or such larger number as the Commission may from time to time determine.

7. The proceedings of the Commission shall not be invalidated by any vacancy in the membership of the Commission or by any defect in the appointment of any member thereof.

8. If at any meeting of the Commission the votes are equally divided on any question, the person acting as chairman of the meeting shall have a second or casting vote.

9. The Commission shall refer to one or more of their number for report and recommendation such matters as may be determined by the Commission and shall delegate to one or more of their number such of the functions conferred on the Commission by this Act, to such extent and subject to such conditions or restrictions, as may with the approval of the Secretary of State be so determined.

10. In any application or other proceeding coming before them the Commission may order that the evidence shall be taken on oath.

11. Subject to the foregoing provisions of this Schedule, the Commission shall have power to regulate their own procedure.

Office, Officers and Servants

12. The Commission shall have an office in the crofting counties at which communications and notices will at all times be received.

13. The Secretary of State may provide the services of such officers and servants as the Commission may require.

Instruments executed or issued by the Commission

14. The application of the seal of the Commission to any document shall be attested by at least one member of the Commission and by the person for the time being acting as secretary to the Commission.

15. Every document purporting to be an instrument issued by the Commission and to be sealed and attested as aforesaid or to be duly signed on behalf of the Commission shall be received in evidence and shall be deemed to be such an instrument without further proof unless the contrary is shown.

Section 5   SCHEDULE 2

THE STATUTORY CONDITIONS

1. The crofter shall pay his rent at the terms at which it is due and payable.

2. The crofter shall not, except in accordance with the provisions of this Act, execute any deed purporting to assign his tenancy.

3. The crofter shall, by himself or his family, with or without hired labour, cultivate his croft, without prejudice to the right hereby conferred on him to make such use thereof for subsidiary or auxiliary occupations as, in case of dispute, the Land Court may find to be reasonable and not inconsistent with the cultivation of the croft.

4. The crofter shall provide such fixed equipment on his croft as may be necessary to enable him to cultivate the croft.

5. The crofter shall not, to the prejudice of the interest of the landlord, persistently injure the croft by the dilapidation of buildings or, after notice in writing has been given by the landlord to the crofter not to commit, or to desist from, the particular injury specified in the notice, by the deterioration of the soil.

6. The crofter shall not sublet his croft or any part thereof otherwise than with the consent in writing of the Commission and in accordance with such conditions (which shall not include conditions relating to rent) as the Commission in giving their consent may impose:

Provided that nothing in this paragraph shall be construed as debarring a crofter from subletting any dwelling-house or other building forming part of his croft to holiday visitors.

7. The crofter shall not, except in accordance with the provisions of this Act, subdivide his croft.

8. The crofter shall not, without the consent in writing of the landlord, erect or suffer to be erected on the croft any dwelling-house otherwise than in substitution for a dwelling-house which at the commencement of this Act was already on the croft:

Provided that, if at the commencement of this Act there was no dwelling-house on the croft, the crofter may erect one dwelling-house thereon.

9. The crofter shall not persistently violate any written condition signed by him for the protection of the interest of the landlord or of neighbouring crofters which is legally applicable to the croft and which the Land Court shall find to be reasonable.

10. The crofter shall not do any act whereby he becomes apparently insolvent within the meaning of the Bankruptcy (Scotland) Act 1985.

11. The crofter shall permit the landlord or any person authorised by the landlord in that behalf to enter upon the croft for the purpose of exercising (subject always to the payment of such compensation as in case of dispute the Land Court may find to be reasonable in respect of any damage done or occasioned thereby) any of the following rights, and shall not obstruct the landlord or any person authorised as aforesaid in the exercise of any of such rights, that is to say—

(a) mining or taking minerals, or digging or searching for minerals;
(b) quarrying or taking stone, marble, gravel, sand, clay, slate or other workable mineral;
(c) using for any estate purpose any springs of water rising on the croft and not required for the use thereof;
(d) cutting or taking timber or peats, excepting timber and other trees planted by the crofter or any of his predecessors in the tenancy, or which may be necessary for ornament or shelter, and excepting also such peats as may be required for the use of the croft;
(e) opening or making roads, fences, drains and water courses;
(f) passing and re-passing to and from the shore of the sea or any loch with or without vehicles for the purpose of exercising any right of property or other right belonging to the landlord;
(g) viewing or examining at reasonable times the state of the croft and all buildings or improvements thereon;
(h) hunting, shooting, fishing or taking game or fish, wild birds or vermin;

but nothing in this paragraph shall be held to preclude the crofter from recovering any compensation for damage by game which is recoverable under section 52 of the Agricultural Holdings (Scotland) Act 1991, by a tenant, and that section shall apply accordingly, with the substitution, however, of the Land Court for arbitration.

12. The crofter shall not on his croft, without the consent in writing of the landlord, open any house for the sale of intoxicating liquors.

13. In this Schedule—

"cultivate" includes the use of a croft for horticulture or for any purpose of husbandry, including the keeping or breeding of livestock, poultry or bees, the growing of fruit, vegetables and the like and the planting of trees and use of the land as woodlands;

"game" means deer, hares, rabbits, pheasants, partridges, grouse, blackgame, capercailzie, ptarmigan, woodcock, snipe, wild duck, widgeon and teal.

Section 30(7)   SCHEDULE 3

PERMANENT IMPROVEMENTS

1. Dwelling-house.
2. Improvement works carried out in compliance with a notice of a final resolution served under Part IV of the Housing (Scotland) Act 1987.
3. Farm offices.
4. Subsoil and other drains.
5. Walls and fences.
6. Deep trenching.
7. Clearing the ground.
8. Planting trees, other than under section 48(4) of this Act.

9. Making piers or landing stages.

10. Roads practicable for vehicles from the croft to the public road or the sea shore.

11. All other improvements which, in the judgment of the Land Court, will add to the value of the croft as an agricultural subject.

12. Buildings or other structures erected under section 5 of the Crofters (Scotland) Act 1961 or section 31 of this Act, being buildings or structures which are fixtures on the land, or works executed under the said section 5 or 31.

Section 38(7)   SCHEDULE 4

CONFIRMATION AND VALIDITY OF REORGANISATION SCHEMES

PART I

Procedure for confirming reorganisation schemes

1. Before confirming a reorganisation scheme the Secretary of State shall—

(a) serve on every owner and every occupier of land to which the draft scheme applies a copy of the draft scheme together with a notice naming a place within the locality in which such land is situated where a copy of the maps and plans submitted with the draft scheme may be inspected at all reasonable hours and stating that such owner or occupier may, within 28 days from the date of the service of the notice, object in such manner as may be specified in the notice to the draft scheme or to any provision contained therein; and

(b) in two successive weeks publish in one or more newspapers circulating in the locality in which the land to which the scheme applies is situated a notice stating that the draft scheme has been submitted to him, specifying the land to which the scheme applies, naming a place within the locality where a copy of the draft scheme and of the maps and plans submitted therewith may be inspected at all reasonable hours, and stating that any person having an interest in any land to which the scheme applies may, within 28 days from the date of the first publication of the notice, object in such manner as may be specified in the notice to the draft scheme or to any provision contained therein.

2. If no objection is made under paragraph 1 of this Schedule or if all objections so made are withdrawn, the Secretary of State may, subject to the provisions of paragraph 4 of this Schedule, confirm the draft scheme with or without modifications.

3. If any objection made as aforesaid is not withdrawn, the Secretary of State shall, before deciding whether to confirm the draft scheme, cause a public local inquiry to be held, and after considering the objection and the report of the person who held the inquiry the Secretary of State may, if he thinks fit and subject to the provisions of paragraph 4 of this Schedule, confirm the draft scheme with or without modifications.

4. Where the Secretary of State proposes to make any modification in the draft scheme by virtue either of paragraph 2 or 3 of this Schedule, he shall, before deciding to confirm the draft scheme as so modified, serve on each of the persons referred to in sub-paragraph (a) of paragraph 1 of this Schedule and on any other person who is in his opinion may be substantially affected by such modification a notice specifying the modification and stating that such person may, within 14 days from the date of the service of the notice, make representations in writing concerning the modification to the Secretary of State, and the Secretary of State shall consider any representations so made before he decides whether to confirm the draft scheme as so modified.

5. Notwithstanding anything in paragraph 3 of this Schedule, the Secretary of State may require any person who has made an objection to state in writing the grounds thereof and may disregard the objection for the purposes of this Schedule if it is an objection which in the opinion of the Secretary of State is frivolous, or which relates exclusively to the assessment of any sum which will fall to be fixed under this Act or any other enactment by the Land Court, or which relates to the assessment of compensation on the compulsory acquisition of land or of an interest in land by virtue of section 39 of this Act.

6. Subsections (2) to (8) of section 210 of the Local Government (Scotland) Act 1973 (which relate to the holding of local inquiries) shall apply in relation to a public local inquiry held under paragraph 3 of this Schedule as they apply in relation to local inquiries held under the said section 210.

PART II

Validity of reorganisation schemes

7. On confirming a reorganisation scheme the Secretary of State shall forthwith—

(a) serve on every person on whom a notice was required to be served under sub-paragraph

(a) of paragraph 1 or paragraph 4 of this Schedule a notice stating that the scheme has been confirmed; and

(b) publish in one or more newspapers circulating in the locality in which the land to which the scheme applies is situated a notice stating that the scheme has been confirmed and naming a place within the locality where a copy of the scheme and of the maps and plans relating thereto may be inspected at all reasonable hours.

(8) If any person aggrieved by a reorganisation scheme desires to question its validity on the ground that it is not within the powers of this Act or that any requirement of this Act has not been complied with, he may, within 6 weeks from the date of the first publication of the notice referred to in paragraph 7(b) of this Schedule, make an application for the purpose to the Court of Session, and if any such application is made the Court, if satisfied that the scheme is not within the powers of this Act or that the interests of the applicant have been substantially prejudiced by a failure to comply with any requirement of this Act, may quash the scheme either generally or in so far as it affects any property or interest of the applicant; but except as aforesaid the scheme shall not at any time be questioned in any proceedings whatsoever.

Sections 19(1), 43(4) and (6),   SCHEDULE 5
45(2) and 46(3)

PROVISIONS AS TO SECURITY, ETC., OF LOANS

1. The loan shall be secured by a heritable security over the land in favour of the Secretary of State.

2. The loan shall either be repaid by half-yearly instalments of principal with such interest and within such period (not exceeding such period as may be fixed by the Treasury) from the date of the loan, or at such date thereafter not exceeding 18 months as may be agreed on, or shall be repaid with such interest and within such period by a terminable annuity payable by half-yearly instalments.

3. The amount for the time being unpaid may at any time be discharged, and any such terminable annuity may at any time be redeemed in accordance with tables fixed by the Secretary of State.

4. A certificate by the Secretary of State that the whole of the loan has been repaid or that such terminable annuity has been redeemed shall, without any other instrument, operate as a discharge of the loan or extinction of the terminable annuity, as the case may be, and the recording of such certificate in the Register of Sasines or the registration of the certificate in the Land Register of Scotland shall be equivalent to the recording or the registration of a discharge of the said heritable security.

5. The Secretary of State shall cause to be prepared and duly recorded all documents necessary for securing the payment of any loan over land made by him, and shall include in the loan the cost so incurred, or to be incurred, in accordance with scales set forth in tables fixed by the Secretary of State.

Section 63(1)   SCHEDULE 6

TRANSITIONAL PROVISIONS AND SAVINGS

1. In so far as anything done under an enactment repealed by this Act could have been done under a corresponding provision of this Act, it shall not be invalidated by the repeal but shall have effect as if done under that provision.

2. Where any period of time specified in an enactment repealed by this Act is current at the commencement of this Act, this Act shall have effect as if the corresponding provision thereof had been in force when that period began to run.

3. Any reference in any enactment or document, whether express or implied, to an enactment repealed by this Act shall, unless the context otherwise requires, be construed as a reference to the corresponding enactment in this Act.

4. Nothing in this Act shall affect the enactments repealed by this Act in their operation in relation to offences committed before the commencement of this Act.

5. The repeal by this Act of section 22 of the 1955 Act shall not affect the operation of that section in so far as it relates to a person who is the owner and occupier of a holding mentioned in subsection (6) of that section.

6. Notwithstanding the repeal by this Act of section 3 of the Crofter Forestry (Scotland) Act 1991, the amendments made by that section to section 1 of the Forestry Act 1979 and to section 2 of the Farm Land and Rural Development Act 1988 shall continue to have the same effect as they had immediately before the commencement of this Act.

Section 63(2)   SCHEDULE 7

REPEALS

PART I

ENACTMENTS REPEALED SO FAR AS THEY APPLY IN THE CROFTING COUNTIES

Chapter	Short title	Extent of repeal
49 & 50 Vict. c. 29	The Crofters (Scotland) Act 1886	Section 30. Section 33.
1 & 2 Geo. 5 c. 49	The Small Landholders (Scotland) Act 1911	Section 28.
1976 c. 21	The Crofting Reform (Scotland) Act 1976	Section 17(2).

PART II

OTHER ENACTMENTS REPEALED

Chapter	Short title	Extent of repeal
3 & 4 Eliz. 2 c. 21	The Crofters (Scotland) Act 1955	The whole Act.
9 & 10 Eliz. 2 c. 58	The Crofters (Scotland) Act 1961	The whole Act.
1976 c. 21	The Crofting Reform (Scotland) Act 1976	The whole Act except section 17.
1985 c. 73	The Law Reform (Miscellaneous Provisions) (Scotland) Act 1985	Sections 30 and 31.
1991 c. 18	The Crofter Forestry (Scotland) Act 1991	The whole Act.

TABLE OF DERIVATIONS

SHOWING THE DERIVATION OF THE PROVISIONS OF THE BILL

Note: The following abbreviations are used in this Table:—

1955	=	The Crofters (Scotland) Act 1955 (c.21)
1961	=	The Crofters (Scotland) Act 1961 (c.58)
1968	=	The Law Reform (Miscellaneous Provisions) (Scotland) Act 1968 (c.70)
1973	=	The Local Government (Scotland) Act 1973 (c.65)
1974	=	The Housing (Scotland) Act 1974 (c.45)
1975	=	The Criminal Procedure (Scotland) Act 1975 (c.21)
1976	=	The Crofting Reform (Scotland) Act 1976 (c.21)
1985	=	The Law Reform (Miscellaneous Provisions) (Scotland) Act 1985 (c.73)
1991	=	The Crofter Forestry (Scotland) Act 1991 (c.18)
R (followed by a number)	=	The recommendation so numbered in the Appendix to the Report of the Scottish Law Commission.

Provisions	Derivations
1	1955 s.1; 1961 s.1; 1976 Sch. 2 para. 4.
2	1955 s.2; 1976 Sch. 2 para. 5.
3	1955 s.3(1), (2), (5) and (6); 1961 Sch. 1 Pt. II para. 9; 1976 s.14.

Provisions	Derivations
4(1)	1961 s.2(2).
(2)	1961 s.2(2A); 1976 Sch. 2 para. 17.
(3)	1961 s.2(3).
(4)	1961 s.2(5).
5(2)	1955 s.3(3).
(3)	1955 s.3(4).
6	1955 s.5.
7	1955 s.7; 1961 Sch. 1 Pt. I para. 1.
8	1955 s.8; 1961 Sch. 1 Pt. II para. 10; 1968 Sch. 2 Pt. I para. 1; 1976 s.15 and Sch. 2 para. 6.
9	1955 s.9.
10	1955 s.10; 1968 Sch. 2 Pt. I paras. 2 and 3.
11	1955 s.11; 1968 s.8 Sch. 2 Pt. II.
12(1)–(4)	1976 s.1, R1.
(5)	1955 s.28(4); 1976 s.21.
13	1976 s.2.
14	1976 s.3.
15	1976 s.4.
16	1976 s.5.
17	1976 s.6; R2.
18	1976 s.7.
19	1976 s.8; Enterprise and New Towns (Scotland) Act 1990 (c.35) s.22.
20	1955 s.12; 1961 Sch. 1 Pt. II para. 11; 1976 Sch. 3; 1985 s.30(1); 1991 s.2(1).
21	1976 s.9; 1985 s.30(2); R3.
22	1955 s.17; 1976 Sch. 2 para. 9.
23	1955 s.16; 1961 Sch. 1 Pt. I para. 5 & Pt. II para. 12; 1968 Sch. 2 Pt. I para. 17; 1975 ss.289F and 289G; 1976 s.13 Sch. 2 para. 8; R4.
24	1955 ss.12(4), 16(7), (9) and (9A).
25	1955 s.16A; 1976 s.13(3).
26	1955 s.13; 1961 Sch. 1 Pt. I para. 3.
27	1961 s.11.
28(1) to (16)	1961 s.12; 1976 Sch. 2 para. 20.
(17)	1961 s.19(2).
29	1961 s.13; 1976 Sch. 2 para. 21.
30(1)	1955 s.14(1); 1968 s.8 Sch. 2 Pt. II.
(2)	1955 s.14(2).
(3)	1955 s.14(3).
(4)	1955 s.14(8).
(5)	1955 s.14(10).
(6)	1955 s.14(11).
(7)	1955 s.37(1).
31	1961 s.5.
32	1961 s.6; 1968 Sch. 2 paras. 19 to 21.
33	1955 s.6.
34(1)	1955 s.14(6).
(2)	1955 s.14(7).
(3)	1955 s.14(8).
35	1955 s.14(9).
36	1955 s.28; 1961 Sch. 1 Pt. I para. 7.
37	1976 s.10.
38	1961 s.8.
39	1961 s.9.
40	1955 s.15; 1975 ss.289F and 289G; 1976 Sch. 2 para. 7.
41	1961 s.3; 1976 Sch. 2 para. 18; 1991 s.2(7).
42(1) to (6) and (8) to (10)	1955 s.22; 1961 s.14; 1975 ss.289F and 289G; 1976 s.12(2), (5) and (6); 1985 s.31. R5(a) and (b).
(7)	1961 s.14(2).
43	1955 s.23; 1957 s.10(7).
44	1955 s.28(3).
45	1976 s.12(1), (3), (4) and (5).
46(1) to (3)	1955 s.31; 1976 s.12(2) and (5); 1976 Sch. 2 para. 13.

Provisions	Derivations
46(4)	1961 s.14(1).
47(1) to (9)	1955 s.24; 1961 15(1), Sch. 1 Pt. II para. 13; 1976 s.16(1).
(10)	1961 s.15(6).
48	1955 s.25; 1961 Sch. 1 Pt. II para. 14; 1976 s.16(2) and (3); 1991 ss.1(1) and 2(2).
49	1955 s.26; 1961 s.15(2) and (3) Sch. 1 Pt. II para. 15; 1976 s.16(4); 1991 s.2(3).
50	1991 s.1(2).
51	1961 s.2(4) and (5).
52 (except subs (6))	1955 s.27; 1961 s.15; 1975 ss.289F and 289G; 1976 s.16(5) and Sch. 2 para. 11; 1991 s.2(4); R6(a) and (b).
(6)	1961 s.15(5).
53(1)	1961 s.4(1); 1976 Sch. 2 para. 19.
(2)	1961 s.4(2).
54	1976 s.17(2).
55	1955 s.29.
56	1955 s.30; 1975 ss.289E, 289F and 289G.
57	1955 s.32; 1963 s.47.
58	1955 s.33.
59	1955 s.35.
60	1955 s.36.
61	1955 s.37; 1961 s.17(1); 1973 Sch. 27 Pt. II para. 20; 1976 s.21.
62	1955 s.38; 1976 s.19.
Sch. 1	1955 Sch. 1; 1976 s.18.
Sch. 2	1955 Sch. 2; 1961 Sch. 1 Pt. II para. 20; 1991 s.2(5).
Sch. 3	1955 Sch. 5; 1961 Sch. 1 Pt. II para. 21; 1974 s.25(3); 1991 s.2(6).
Sch. 4	1961 Sch. 2; 1973 s.237(2).
Sch. 5	1955 Sch. 3; 1976 Sch. 2 para. 15.

INDEX